Building an entrepreneurial culture from the strategic modeling

Dougglas Hurtado Carmona. Fernando Suarez Galvis. Jorge Vengoechea Orozco

Building an entrepreneurial culture from the strategic modeling

Building an entrepreneurial culture from the strategic modeling

Dougglas Hurtado Carmona
Fernando Suarez Galvis
Jorge Vengoechea Orozco

ISBN (Print): **978-1-387-94687-7**
ISBN (Epub): **978-1-387-94652-5**

©2022 Copyright.
First edition

Cover page:
Adapted from content depositphotos # 186937186 © AndreyPopov

Authors

Douglas Hurtado Carmona
Doctor in Innovation Management. Doctoral candidate in Educational Technology from the Mar de Cortés University Center. Master's degree in Systems and Computer Engineering, Systems Engineer, Universidad del Norte. Researcher and writer. He was Dean of the Faculty of Systems Engineering.

Fernando Suarez Galvis
Doctor of Administration. Master in Business Administration. Specialization in Economics. Professional in Economic Sciences. teacher and researcher

Jorge Luis Vengoechea Orozco
Doctor in Innovation Management. Master of Business Administration University of Louisville, Systems Engineer, Cisco Networking Academy Program Instructor, Research Professor Metropolitan University of Barranquilla. Academic Advisor. He was Dean of the Faculty of Economic and Administrative Sciences.

CONTENT

Introduction

Building a culture of entrepreneurship from strategic modeling, contributes to directing efforts in the selected path, guaranteeing results in the short and medium term. This statement is based on the implications of the term, since, when speaking of strategic modeling, it necessarily refers to the exercise carried out by business organizations or not, in order to define both the strategies and the tactical actions required to develop in a manner effective management to be carried out.

Therefore, it is essential to specify the model and prioritize the strategies with the aim of achieving greater viability at the time of reaching the proposed goals. In this sense, the initiatives that some university institutions have taken with the development of an entrepreneurial culture, even when it has not given the expected results, due to ignorance or little use, are of vital importance for the public university institutions of the municipality of Soledad Atlántico, organizations that have expressed interest in the continuous improvement and quality of all their processes.

Therefore, when considering that strategic modeling is based on analysis and a dose of intuition, it represents a point of equilibrium in the processes, due to its flexibility to allow and at certain times force modifications in what is planned in order to respond to the changes that may occur Regarding what has been expressed, the interest in the subject and the practice of entrepreneurship in Barranquilla, in the last two decades, is a consequence of the unemployment of a portion of the population, but also of the search for new work options outside the State and traditional private companies. Beyond the entrepreneurship promoted from the industrialized countries, in the country the reflection on the economic initiatives of the population is gradually taking effect.

There is a sector of the population that, when undertaking, tends to do so based on oversized projects, seeking quick results, with little awareness of costs and a very limited management of adversities, hence the need to formulate guidelines that can guide efficiently and effectively. effective this process, being the university institutions the organizations par excellence to do so. Hence, in this work the study of aspects that support each of the analyzed elements is deepened, in order to specify the proposed purpose, which is directed at the construction of an entrepreneurial culture from strategic modeling, which integrates the actions required to position the public university institutions of the municipality of Soledad Atlántico in the socio-community environment.

In this sense, the book that is presented is structured in seven chapters, through which a journey is made through all the events of the research that supports this socialization. Starting with an approach to the reality of the events, where the motivation to develop this work and what the reality is addressed is explained. Immediately a review of previous experiences is made to know the state of the art of the analyzed categories. In the next chapter, we analyze what refers to the culture of entrepreneurship to continue with entrepreneurship.

Later, in Chapter V the content of strategic planning is developed until reaching strategic modeling. Continuing with a review of the methodological path. Then you get to the point of the expected results, to later enter the Epilogue. The suggestions are presented below, where the recommended strategic guidelines are formulated, closing with the bibliographic references that support the work presented.

Finally, we invite all those interested in the subject, to read the contents outlined here.

Chapter One: Approach to the reality of the facts

For many years there have been variations that affect university institutions, directly influencing the structure and dynamics of education, which generates conjunctural situations depending on the environment and other influencing elements in the strategic actions of this type of organization. Due to this situation, strategies possibly not aligned to the intentions prevail, whose objective is to achieve the desired purposes, to survive those elements or factors that affect their management, not counting the new changing way of looking at people within the organization as leaders in each of the processes or functions that it develops or works within them.

In this sense, the changes caused have contributed to the progress of strategies, with new approaches to directing management in university organizations. In addition to the fact that many of the Rectors of these institutions, for fear of the risks caused by the changes, prefer to continue with the applications of the strategies already known, which produces a culture of resistance to change, for the improvements of the given functions , contributing to the success of these, due to the challenges to be faced in current times regarding how it is structured and implemented in this type of companies in the education sector, this context is generally given by the Latin American countries that perpetuate their mission, to guarantee performance from the social to the ethical. On the other hand,

It supports what is expressed by Gibb and Hannom (2007) when they point out that the variations presented by the pressures of globalization in economic systems lead to considerable care by policy makers around the world, whose objective is to promote education related to entrepreneurship, taking into account the social divergences that generate changes in the environments by the different educational entities, the governments and private and public organizations of the Latin American countries, seeking to seek changes in higher education; coupled with entrepreneurship.

The first indications on the subject of entrepreneurship began in 1947 in the Colombian context, making possible the incursion of the first courses of knowledge in relation to teaching and learning, in reality despite the aforementioned date, the Entrepreneurship has been working in recent years where there is concern by higher education institutions on the subject in relation to the field of knowledge, in which they try to understand the entrepreneur in a systemic way, examining their impacts on business processes.

Likewise, with the disclosure of Law 1014, January 2, 2006, the progress of a culture in entrepreneurship is strengthened, whose characterization is to train entrepreneurs in all areas of knowledge,in order to implement an entrepreneurial culture in the different organizations with specific activities in the market, with the aim of developing in individuals skills to be competitive in the areas where they operate, whether these are labor, citizen or business skills, which are forged within a formal education system and in those cases where training is non-formal in order to incorporate people into the productive sector.that are forged within a formal education system and in those cases where the training is of a non-formal nature in order to incorporate people into the productive sector.that are forged within a formal education system and in those cases where the training is of a non-formal nature in order to incorporate people into the productive sector.

In this sense, one of the main challenges that is presented in the universities is precisely the traditional teaching system that they have imparted to students; whose attributes are reflected in the different characterizations of every entrepreneur, therefore, it is a valuable input for any organization, be it in education or any other level of productive activity.

In this sense, one of the main problems of university institutions is that there are probably actions coming from strategic plans, but that they are separated even belonging to the same department, but subdivided by sub-department with specific plans and an equal purpose. This possibly occurs in any organization, because individuals think individually and not collectively, making it difficult to align their actions with the purpose of creating cultural habits over time.

According to the Ministry of Commerce, Industry and Tourism, as well as the Colombian Association of Universities (2014), all these situations have caused limitations to teaching and learning to direct a direction, with respect to administrative processes and especially in the didactic To build an entrepreneurial spirit in the environment, among students in training institutions (IES), for this reason those economic efforts and commitments made by universities are inefficiently outlined, whose real objective is to pursue an entrepreneurial culture.

On the other hand, as a result of an empirical observation by the researcher in the Universities located in the city of Barranquilla, it was possible to show a limitation in the development of competitiveness, due to the lack of resources from the government and other stimuli that help to promote the development of ideas through technological implementations, access to flexible credits, among others; It is important to highlight that not only these elements contribute to slowing down the process of implementing an entrepreneurial culture in these organizations, but also the general demotivation of all the collaborators who execute the service. For this reason, it is necessary to involve everyone in decision-making, integrating communication,

However, the management implemented in the actions without good communication becomes inefficient, in the development of labor practices, above all, in the emergence of new ideas that favor the members of the organization, due to the lack of good channels of communication. communication.

From what has been said, it is inferred that by not implementing a good strategy for the development of actions in correspondence with the purposes desired by each Institution, with regard to teaching and learning implemented according to the programs approved by the governing body of the process, which It must be based on the purposes established according to the organization and the impact it intends to cause to the students, on the importance of the subject in their training, to achieve changes in structure and seek results that are visible in the organization.

In correspondence with what has been stated, the Ministry of Education (2015) refers to the fact that, in some university institutions, there is possibly abandonment in the continuity of resource management, due to financial and economic lack, element this, of extremely important when starting a strategic plan or designing strategies that add sustainability and permanence to the actions aimed at strategic direction.

On the other hand, most universities have a model of strategies to direct their actions, with which they intend to achieve the established objectives, implementing a culture over time in order to create ethical and moral habits for good performance, The idea is that they always pursue goals by means of measurement indicators, in order to maintain a high quality in training and give it sustainability if it is accredited, this is how the institutions seek to possibly generate settlements of culture but with an ingredient of utmost relevance is entrepreneurial thinking.

In this sense, it is perceived that Higher Education organizations in the city of Barranquilla seek to build an entrepreneurial culture from a strategic modeling, in order to be more competitive, however, in privately managed universities, the The fact of establishing without much bureaucracy the necessary budget to generate stimulus among the people who are within them, not so in those of public management because they depend on a budget approved by the educational authority.

All these situations, in a certain way, hinder the making of correct decisions, being one of the elements that most transgresses the collaborator, due to the fact that they do not have enough information, which makes the individual probably ineffective in their efforts, affecting in a relevant way their management in the labor practice, a consequence of not being clear about the information of the strategies implemented in the HEI, with ignorance of the strategies designed by the organization and possibly even more serious, they are unaware of the strategies designed by their department, or by their faculty in the case of HE institutions.

This does not happen only in Colombia, there are also other countries such as Mexico where this issue began to be introduced, since the employment index showed contraction, hence the decision was made to motivate people to create and start new companies to offer jobs and create further business development. Starting from that undertaking, in a broad sense, aims to make decisions with some risk; in a more restricted sense, to create companies, where the risk is greater. In both cases, economic approaches that the school can awaken, encourage or strengthen.

Chapter Two: Review of previous experiences

Busto et al (2008) cited by Robles and Pelekais (2015), published an article entitled "Beyond strategic management in Higher Education: Application of the Balanced Scorecard", in which the strategic tools were identified as an instrument, whose This objective is characterized by strategic plans as models for the use of platforms in which the performance of the University is measured.

The study was carried out at the Universidad de la Fronteras, together with several universities from the different cities in Colombia, which was developed under an analysis carried out through the behavior of people, in order to identify the different types of strategies, who established a series of indicators, in which the performance is described and the dispersion of thoughts in the actions is concluded, with respect to the purposes to be achieved. In this sense, allusion is made to the use of the CMI Balanced Scorecard, with a field study, seeking the competitive advantages necessary to stay in the market (Service and Development for Education).

Galindo and Echeverría (2011) wrote an article entitled "Diagnosis of the entrepreneurial culture in the School of Engineering of Antioquia". Because of this, the Entrepreneurship area identified the need to promote an entrepreneurial culture in the community, for which it was required, first of all, to diagnose its existence. Initially, a theoretical tour was carried out in order to standardize the concepts of culture, entrepreneurship and entrepreneurial culture, which allowed the authors to identify the six components of the entrepreneurial spirit that were evaluated: way of thinking, reasoning and acting centered on the opportunities; consideration of risk; creativity and innovation; generation of value; proactivity, and search for information.

These components were analyzed from surveys and in-depth interviews, to identify the perceptions that community members had about them, which resulted in the EIA community having said components at different levels of development. Recommending as future work to carry out the periodic diagnosis of the entrepreneurial culture in order to validate the progress in its development.

Complementing what has been said, Del Pilar (2011) in his article "Education in entrepreneurship: strengthening of Entrepreneurial Competence at the Pontificia Universidad Javeriana Cali", carry out a study on the strengthening of curricula in entrepreneurship in universities, as a proposal of the university model with the aim to strengthen entrepreneurial skills, which implicitly carries a series of characterizations to define the culture of individuals in the organization and also contribute to strengthening teaching - learning, which complements the methodology for creating ideas.

Concluding that, at the Javeriana University, through the application of curricular studies, the transversality of entrepreneurship is implemented, in order to create a competitive development culture and the training of students, making changes in people's habits, through their daily work.

For his part, Pérez (2011) conducted an investigation entitled "Entrepreneurship as a managerial strategy in educational institutions", which aimed to analyze entrepreneurship as a managerial strategy in educational institutions in Barranquilla, Colombia. Based on a descriptive research framed in its design in a transactional non-experimental field study, the observation study technique was used by survey and the questionnaire directed to the conventional Likert-type scale was used as an instrument, as for the validity of the instrument. the evidence related to the content through the opinion of five experts in the area of education.

In relation to the results obtained, they show that the public educational institutions of the city of Barranquilla, Colombia, are tutored by pro-active, innovative, entrepreneurial people, showing organizational leadership, obtaining skills to generate a quality education, due to this recommends holding a training workshop in order to strengthen entrepreneurial activities that allow you to be proactive, creative and especially having self-control.

Bracho (2013) worked on a presentation that he presented at the VII National and IV International Research Conference of the URBE, entitled "Entrepreneurship: Tool for Innovation and Competitiveness". The main objective was focused on exploring the concepts of entrepreneurship as a driver of innovation and competitiveness in socio-productive environments, a tool to strengthen social capital through the consolidation of business ideas as job-generating alternatives, based on satisfy the needs of regional and national contexts obtaining quality of life.

The systemic search was carried out by indexed databases, in scientific documents related to the variable. To collect the information, a matrix with fundamental aspects, typologies and similar elements was analyzed. Inferring, that to innovate the human component is relevant, which must be open, flexible and adaptable. For this reason, government entities must establish public policies for the endogenous progress of organized groups, that is, citizens with vision, transforming agents of the producer apparatus.

To which divergent practices are required to instruct training programs in skills and attitudes oriented to the participatory, permanent, comprehensive construction of citizens committed to socio-economic advancement, where emerging activities are visualized, conceptualized and implemented from a leading foundation, maintaining In tune with society to determine the skills that should be expanded in a bank of eligible as a key element for the implementation of proactive markets, entrepreneurship as a tool for competitiveness and innovation, must move from the paradigm of the orthodox towards that of technologies social.

Chirinos (2013) also presented a presentation called "Sustainable Entrepreneurship as State Policy" at the VII National and IV International Research Conference of URBE. This study is documentary in nature, it presents different theories regarding sustainable entrepreneurship, where the main characteristic is economic and social innovation as a fundamental pillar for its development, it is seen as an alternative to change the living conditions of women. people contributing significantly to collective benefits, aiming at socio-economic development, converting opportunities into goods and services to satisfy citizens' needs, incorporating education as a stimulating mechanism to promote sustainable business initiatives, thereby transforming society,

For this, the purpose of establishing a political agenda is considered where the design of public policies is contemplated, which provides a specific fiscal legal framework oriented to sustainable entrepreneurship without restrictions with full freedom for its exercise.

The plurinational state of Bolivia (2013), in collaboration with the United Nations Development Program, funded by ICCO Civil Society and Melting Pot Bolivia, developed a project on the "Promotion of Youth Entrepreneurship in the city of El Alto" BOL / 87104 ".

To this end, the project was fundamentally oriented to the development of a management model for youth enterprises, aimed at addressing the problem of the lack of markets, which can serve as input for the execution of strategies, actions and policies of the Ministry of Labor and in general from public or private institutions related to employment and productive development.

The model is based on new approaches to entrepreneurship and innovation and sought to promote positive changes in entrepreneurial skills and mentality as a basis for creating value, comprehensive sustainability and social well-being. The initial formulation of the model was enriched through the pilot experience, reaching a final version that collects the lessons learned, needs, and characteristics of the target population.

The accompanying pilot experience was developed for a period of 10 months and focused on young people between 18 and 35 years old with ongoing ventures (MyPE) (1-4 years), mainly in the productive sector. The support axes rest on two pillars: the agile entrepreneurship approach and the development of personal capacities. Additionally, technical assistance and administrative capacity strengthening activities are contemplated.

The main achievements of the initiative include: The formulation of a new business management model adapted to the Bolivian reality;

the strengthening of capacities and entrepreneurial mentality in the young people of the pilot experience.

On the other hand, in a Report made by Redemprender (2014) cited by Robles and Pelekais (2015) as a result of their research entitled "Re-entrepreneurship", the importance of entrepreneurship in innovation is analyzed. The results show the need to direct the efforts of the organization (Redemprender), in order to support the constant cyclical and dynamic actions in entrepreneurship and innovation; Among the terms of support, it makes known the necessary and training resources that contribute to the knowledge to understand and understand the different characters of the university.

The research was supported by practical studies carried out in different Colombian, Chilean and Portuguese universities, with a total of 108 key informants in each of the organizations, working with a sample with different characteristics in determining the time and purposes, due to the number of participants.

For their part, Rojas et al (2015) in the entitled "Strategies for the Promotion of Entrepreneurship Culture Universities of Valledupar, Colombia", explain the implementation of a mechanism to facilitate planning, in order to stimulate strategies for entrepreneurship by means of a characterization of administrative strategies. Relying on: the Ministry of Industry and Tourism and the Colombian Association of Universities (2014), Congress of Colombia (2006), 100 Good University Entrepreneurship Practices (2012).

The article was the product of an investigation carried out under a qualitative method, through a content analysis of the interviews that were applied in three universities in the municipality of Valledupar (Colombia), the data obtained demonstrate administrative strategies and creation of entrepreneurship units , together with the vice-rectory for research and extension. In this sense, the research asserts that 66% raise awareness, formulate business plans, which showed 40% tertiary sector, 51% secondary sector of a total of 173 business plans.

Hernández and Arano (2015) developed a study on the "development of entrepreneurial culture in university students to strengthen business vision". In the article resulting from this research, the authors affirm that entrepreneurial culture is a concept that has been involved in university students by various organizations, both public and private, in many universities, it is not a topic that is addressed in the different Bachelor's degrees, this concept can be found in the careers of the economic-administrative area, this due to the nature of them, however today and in the face of the problem of lack of employment it is important to work on this concept and try to get students to develop a culture to start a business and promote the opening of sources of employment.

Concluding that the entrepreneurial culture is defined as a way of thinking, reasoning and acting, linked to the search for a business opportunity, which can result in the creation, improvement, realization and renewal of value in the broadest sense of the term, that is to say, not only economic but also social value, and not only for their owners, but also for all the interest groups linked to them such as employees, customers, suppliers and society in general, since a strengthened and growing business generates opportunities for I work not only on the people hired as part of the company's staff, it also generates growth in another business that is the supplier, developing a chain of opportunity and wealth generation.

Ornelas et al (2015) wrote an article on "The entrepreneurial spirit and a factor that influences its early development". In this paper, the authors point out that entrepreneurship is one of the drivers of economic and social development, they continue to affirm that, to base, generate actions and conditions that favor it, it is relevant to study the entrepreneurial spirit, which is understood as the characteristics of the personality that is manifested in the way of thinking and acting linked to the search and use of opportunities.

Although these characteristics are later modified by culture, they are first formed at home, which is why the study contrasts the entrepreneurial spirit of students born to self-employed parents with respect to those of non-self-employed parents, in a sample of 117 students from an Institution of Middle Education of the State of Aguascalientes, Mexico.

Seven dimensions of the entrepreneurial spirit were analyzed: self-confidence, innovative behavior, achievement motivation, emotional self-efficacy, leadership, proactivity and tolerance to uncertainty, finding differences in all dimensions in favor of the children of self-employed mothers, and only in the dimensions of self-confidence and innovative behavior in favor of the children of self-employed parents. The results obtained suggest that the conditions and actions that strengthen the entrepreneurial activity of mothers of families will have a great impact on the development of the entrepreneurial spirit of their children.

Chapter Three: A journey through the culture of entrepreneurship

Entrepreneurship culture is a way of thinking and acting, that is, of internalizing the philosophy that this term represents, which is oriented towards the creation of wealth, through the use of opportunities, the development of a global vision and a fair leadership of what it means to manage a calculated risk, the result of which is the creation of value that benefits everyone equally.

For Hernández et al (2015), citing Alemany and Álvarez (2011), there is no commonly accepted definition of entrepreneurial culture. Some authors consider it a very specific activity, related to the creative destruction of Schumpeter, others have focused on the discovery of opportunities; others have focused on the creation of new companies or the generation of new innovative projects. In general terms, the entrepreneurial culture includes the study of the sources of opportunities, the processes of discovery, evaluation and exploitation of these, and the people who discover, evaluate and innovate them. In addition, although it is not required, the entrepreneurial culture can include the creation of new organizations.

Vidal (2012) in a work developed on the subject, affirms that entrepreneurial people are not alien to the culture, so it is expected that the motivation to undertake is greater if the entrepreneurial activity is socially accepted and the entrepreneurial function is valued and admired. For his part, Cavalli (2007) points out "culture as something that is learned and educated".

In addition, for Martínez-Rodríguez (2008), culture varies over time, so we can affirm that it is a social construction. Hence, when talking about ways of life, customs, values and knowledge that are learned, and that are therefore educable, new lifestyles are developed, even in those social and human groups traditionally not very entrepreneurial, who see In promoting the entrepreneurial spirit, a vital and professional model with which to generate economic development and social cohesion.

For this reason, we speak of culture, calling it entrepreneurial, because it is possible to critically educate citizens to reflect on other alternative growth models to the current one, closer to the principles of social justice, equity and respect for the environment.

In another vein, Ramírez (2005) cited by Hernández et al (2015), affirms that the task of incorporating an entrepreneurial culture in the university is not an easy task since it implies a challenge that represents redesigning the existing educational model, its objectives and strategies to lay the educational and training bases that promote the entrepreneurial mentality of the students, considering in this the intervention of other agents of change and new roles that would allow them to meet the challenge imposed by society that demands greater participation in the process of the economic and social development of the country, to the foregoing must be added the existing predisposition to assume it by its members and especially those who direct it.

On the other hand, the changes that have emerged in the world have been aimed at consolidating a culture of entrepreneurship, which has led educational institutions to promote training through the application of stimuli for the development of entrepreneurial initiatives, based on Policy adaptations in addition to the demands of the environment, with the firm intention of generating new activities and actions that the individual employs to improve their quality of life.

Starting from this, for the Ministry of National Education, of the Republic of Colombia (2010), the culture of entrepreneurship is understood as a set of values, beliefs, ideologies, habits, customs and norms, shared by individuals in the organization and that arise from social interrelation, which generates collective behavior patterns that establish an identity among its members and identify them from another organization.

On the other hand, for the author Pasten (2005), the culture of entrepreneurship is based on the set of values, as well as beliefs and norms, shared within a certain group of people emerged in the social interrelation, where patterns of collective behavior under the identity of its members identifying and differentiating themselves from other groups within companies or institutions. In this regard, it seeks to develop the culture of entrepreneurship in order to employ actions based on the formation of labor, civic and business competencies within the formal and non-formal educational system and its articulation with the productive sector.

In this sense, as stated by Schnarch (2014) citing Rodríguez (2013), promoting a culture of entrepreneurship is preparing the conditions to give way to a responsible initiative and dynamizing the economic system. However, states are aware that short-term policies are not usually sufficient to increase entrepreneurial efficiency, that is, to reduce the failure rate. If one checks the number of institutions and agencies that are dedicated to the promotion and education of economic management worldwide, it is possible to demonstrate the importance of business development services for a culture of entrepreneurship.

On the other hand, when referring to culture in entrepreneurship, the work edited by the Ministry of National Education of Colombia (2011: 10) is cited, who have edited a work on the subject, but emphasizing its context in educational establishments.

To this end, they point out that the culture of entrepreneurship is gradually fostered: at the preschool and basic levels, based on basic and civic competences, the notional and elementary processes of entrepreneurship are worked on; and in secondary education the competencies to promote entrepreneurship are consolidated, as an opportunity for the student to materialize their entrepreneurial attitudes in the development of activities and projects aimed at the creation of companies or business units with a perspective of sustainable development.

Complementing the above, by stating that the process of promoting the culture of entrepreneurship implies the integration of basic and civic competences, entrepreneurship and entrepreneurship to the institutional context, which is manifested by: conceiving it as the result of the construction of the educational project institutional and the life project of its students.

Information that is totally pertinent to the research that supported this work, where the same category is worked but contextualized in higher education. Hence, the criteria of the aforementioned authors are shared, especially when they point out: to develop it intentionally, systematically, providing meaning and relevance to each of the human dimensions: biological, psycho-affective, axiological, political, intellectual, cultural and productive.

Coinciding with Robles and Pelekais (2015), who affirm that the integration of competencies and skills strengthens the experiential area that students can acquire during their training, both at the level of their basic and university education. Hence, the importance of delimiting a strategic model where each of the proposed activities in a specific area are exposed in a planned manner, with their corresponding strategies, actions, goals, deadlines and responsible parties.

Accordingly, Ardenghi (2001) in the context of higher education it is necessary for these organizations to promote the development of skills and characteristics of the entrepreneur, so that from their perspectives they allow taking into account the needs and resources of the actors, with the achievement of innovate and create ideas in companies. It is for this reason, the relevance of entrepreneurship in higher education in relation to the advancement of organizations and not only of them, but of any person.

On the other hand, Ackerman & Cervilla (2007) in their chair of entrepreneurship defines it as a strategy that structures a culture, giving a significant challenge to higher education institutions in regard to training, because it faces factors of character economic, essential element in the motivation of students, so that they are encouraged and discover their entrepreneurial skills, with the intention of exploiting the skills and converting the potential of each individual into opportunities.

In the same way, the HEIs seek the necessary resources to encourage those individuals, who somehow have their skills asleep and do not translate it into the vision of others, in order to create habits over time, contribute to a culture competitive, sustainable organizations, establishing future job contributors, building scenarios to develop their potentials. For this reason, it is necessary to suggest the resources to create scenarios with intentions of innovative ideas, building systemic and continuous environments, for setting objectives and identifying activities in the organization.

Strengthening a culture of entrepreneurship

According to Bermúdez et al (2011), the reinforcement of an entrepreneurial culture can be defined in a series of characterizations, such as social capital. Aspect that supports the success of organizations with the purpose of advancing in competitive development according to the resources they possess, in this case higher education institutions, which are aimed at generating a rapid and high turnaround, taking into account the learning requirements. Likewise, one of the main topics of interest is the economic aspect and this is addressed on the one hand in the reproduction of capital, through entrepreneurship strategies that contribute to the environment.

As established in Law 1014 (2006), the concept of culture is defined as that conjunction of values, habits, beliefs, customs and norms that the individual share in the organization and is born from the interrelation in different environments, whose purpose is reinforce habits in entrepreneurship, together with a collective thinking applying strategies that can be implemented.

For his part, Alemany (2011) defines the reinforcement of an entrepreneurial culture in four aspects that characterize the entrepreneur, such as: autonomy, leadership, innovation and of course development; The first characteristic to be mentioned is the advancement of processes in undertaking ideas through continuous and systemic training of students in their training over time, forging a compulsory education to exercise a culture of the organization in which it can be defined The teaching practice, among the other characteristics, are listed: Autonomy, is a positive way of perceiving things, in addition to the faith and confidence of their aptitudes, thinks of others demonstrating their emotions, among other behaviors typical of an entrepreneurial individual . Thus,

On the other hand, innovation as a third characteristic, the student assumes different aptitudes such as being proactive in the face of new situations in known environments, creating motivation with great ease, taking into account the hierarchy of the moment and the priorities presented, assuming positions with a tendency to resolve problems and even propose improvements.

The fourth characterization mentioned by the author is the leadership or position that the student has before known environmental environments, which wants to direct the actions undertaken and execute them to solve problems, in order to generate well-being for all those who are involved. in the situation.

Hernández et al (2015) complement the above when they point out: the lack of development of an entrepreneurial culture, can result in university graduates trying to be employed and therefore a serious consequence is the lack of employment, and a deterioration in the country's economy, the hope of a government is that society participates by opening sources of employment through new companies.

Academic and research activities that reinforce a culture of entrepreneurship

Regarding this point, RedEmprendia (2014: 8), states:

From the perspective of the substantive functions of a university and the link that is considered to exist between them, the role of research cannot be forgotten. Neither is the relationship between research and training. Teachers carry out a function of disseminating the knowledge generated through research, both for curricular training at the undergraduate or postgraduate level and for follow-up in complementary or extracurricular training activities. In a cyclical way, the work carried out in the postgraduate courses –with a research orientation- will serve to reinforce the research work. On the other hand, research in teaching innovation is essential to advance towards excellence in training or to maintain it. Finally,

Reinforcing what has been raised, it can be affirmed that there are many and varied activities that can be developed in university institutions to strengthen a culture of entrepreneurship, to this end, Gutiérrez (2015: 242) points out:

Research from its different manifestations has begun to receive a response from the different agents interested in its development and results. The echo initially reached contrasts with the linking of companies and the State to give orientation and transit to the initiatives that emerged between them; the possibility of establishing not only alliances, but an organizational structure from which the research triad manages to define the Business Research Competencies Model.

Adding to the above, this situation is transferred to the universities, which, although they have increased their level of presence in the research stages, today and its future show an increase in their exhausted role of transmitting knowledge via content, based on a not very flexible academic structure, in which even the filter of the academic and investigative relationship does not go from the routine production of its own activities to the work of the universities, when despite this, what is done in them must seek application in the environment.

With respect to what was previously referenced by Gutiérrez (2015), Luengo (2003: 16), maintains that:

The reform of knowledge, the reform of thought and the reform of education go hand in hand and are necessary for a reform of society. They are a possibility to regain awareness of our responsibilities as university students, of the relevance of our debate, of our possibilities for action and of our political decisions.

Entrepreneurial organizational learning

According to Lowe and Marriot (2012), the link between individual and organizational learning is a factor that is more critical in entrepreneurial organizations, since from their perception usually the entrepreneur or the entrepreneurial team play a strong role in influencing how the organization it operates, particularly in how knowledge is acquired and applied, in how decisions are made, and in how ambiguity is managed.

To know the way in which learning transcends the individual dimension to become an organizational capacity that is a source of competitive advantage, it is necessary to know the characteristics of a learning organization. Decision making in entrepreneurial organizations

Decisions are influenced by knowledge, context, management styles, and organizational culture. It is therefore pertinent to explore the role that decision-making plays in entrepreneurial organizations. First, it could be argued that organizations that promote learning and anticipate trends would be better prepared to meet the challenges and threats of the business environment. It would not be surprising if such organizations, in their effort to anticipate the future, have considered how to systematically address attention to their opportunities, weaknesses and the exploiting your strengths to take advantage of opportunities.

From this point of view, as Lowe and Marriot (2012) estimate, such apparently objective process occurs in a somewhat different way in entrepreneurial organizations. Drawing on the work of Mintzberg and Westley (2001), these authors describe three ways of approaching decision-making: think first, see first, and do first.

- Think first is defined as the rational process of defining, diagnosing, designing, and deciding. This way would be the least common used, because in practice the decision-making process describes a series of less lengthy steps that go beyond conscious thought.

- Seeing first involves the ability to gain deep intuitive understanding. In-depth knowledge, usually developed through years of experience, followed by an incubation process in which the matter is reflected upon. After that, the moment of result or enlightenment.

- Doing first is the field of pragmatists, who learn as they go. The pragmatist experiments to learn.

In this regard, according to Lowe and Marriot (2012), although individuals can demonstrate a preferred way of approaching decisions, any of the three could be present to a greater or lesser degree. These authors estimate that an entrepreneurial organization here would find an advantage, in the sense that the vision of the entrepreneur and usually his predilection for learning in action serves as a balance to the traditional decision-making process in the corporate sphere.

But, how to promote an entrepreneurial culture?

According to what was proposed by Mestres (2011), the variables that promote the entrepreneurial culture among citizens are many, and it begins by stating the opinion of Trinidad García, a teacher of early childhood education, who affirms: the entrepreneurial spirit can be promoted in school.

In fact, it would be necessary to consider the entrepreneurial culture not only as a specific subject but as a teaching methodology from a transversal perspective. To achieve this, in the first place, it is necessary to solve the deficiencies that education has today: lack of cultural values of the entrepreneurial spirit; ignorance of the opportunities of entrepreneurship and lack of development of business skills.

Afterwards, a change in the didactic methodology should be favored: moving from the traditional style to the entrepreneurial style, the latter understood as more emphasis on practice, proposing negotiated objectives, the student as the center of the learning process, evaluation as an improvement mechanism, among others. aspects of equal importance.

And he adds, in terms of adults and on a personal level, first of all you have to lose your fear of taking risks. If you have a business idea, you can do training courses, read and document yourself, attend conferences, connect with people, other entrepreneurs who help us and show us their way of working, specialize, and even seek professional help in nurseries, chambers of commerce, public administration.

Business success is not a matter of chance or chance but of self-confidence, ingenuity, observation, study and preparation, work, realism and courage. For this reason, it is important to plan, organize, examine and know the market, the economy and our own capacities.

Chapter Four: Strategic Planning

To define the term strategic planning, it is essential to consider the concept of planning. Stoner, Freeman and Gilbert (2006), who indicate that planning involves a process of setting goals and choosing means to achieve those goals.

It is therefore a process that is followed to determine exactly what the organization will do to achieve its objectives. It is understood from the foregoing, that planning is the process of evaluating all relevant information and probable future developments, resulting in a recommended course of action: a plan.

Said plan implies setting objectives and choosing the most appropriate means to achieve them before taking action. From this perspective, planning anticipates decision-making.

In addition to the above, Cuervo (2003) indicates that planning, under the strategic approach, is conceived as a process by which decision-makers in an organization analyze and process information from their internal and external environment, evaluating the different situations related to the organizational performance to anticipate and decide on future directionality.

Therefore, strategic planning is designed to meet the general goals of the organization, while operational planning shows how strategic plans can be applied in daily work.In this sense, strategic planning according to the criteria of Serna (2012) represents the process by which decision-makers in an organization obtain, process and analyze pertinent information, internal and external, in order to evaluate the present situation of the company, as well as its level of competitiveness in order to anticipate and decide on the direction of the institution towards the future.

In the same vein, Sapiro (2010), states that strategic planning is the process that serves to formulate the organization's strategies in order to insert it, according to its mission, in the context in which it is located. This process should not be formal and bureaucratic, but should begin with simple questions such as: What is the current situation in the organization? What is your performance with customers and against competitors? If no changes were made, what would the organization look like one year from now? In two, five or ten years? If the answers to the above questions were not acceptable, what decisions should managers make? What risks would they entail?

Therefore, it is necessary to develop a strategic thinking that according to Garrido (2007), is an elementary principle that fortunately does not go out of style for the human race and is always a good start for any knowledge company, the author continues saying that this position is moves in the axis of institutional, business and professional pragmatics.

Likewise, it is a process through which the environment is evaluated to create corporate strategies aimed at differentiating itself from the competition, thus offering customers something that they cannot obtain anywhere else. This activity, which must be carried out continuously by those in charge of management, in any type of company.

In addition, the aforementioned author refers that this process constitutes a powerful tool with concrete, real and pragmatic effects for the work of the organization. Similarly, it sustains that strategic thinking "is the DNA of strategic planning" (p.68). It also affirms that the work of strategic planning is enriched when it precedes the exercises (collective or individual) of strategic thinking.

For his part, Chiavenato (2010), states that strategic planning is a broad organizational process that implies approval, decision-making and evaluation, seeks to answer basic questions such as why does the organization exist, what it does and how it does it. The result of this process is a plan that serves to guide organizational action in a period of three to five years; and as Ohmae (2004) adds, analysis is the crucial starting point for strategic thinking.

Thus, strategic planning is the resource to achieve what one wants, answering four questions: where were you yesterday? Where am I today?

Where do I want to be tomorrow? And how will I go about achieving it? It is easier to develop a plan than to execute it. The difficult thing is to visualize the future that is desired and from which the present that is needed to achieve it can be built. (Chiavenato, 2010).

According to Testa (2009), planning is developed in two aspects: political (distribution of power) and strategic (ways of putting power into practice). Therefore, for the achievement of planning, there must be full coherence between the political purposes of the state, the methods applied and the actions of organizations or institutions (this requirement is called the Principle of Coherence). In conclusion, strategic planning is not only defining an objective to achieve, but a complex social process that revolves around defined political objectives.

On the other hand, it is important to note that strategic plans and operational plans are linked to the definition of an organization's mission, the general goal that justifies the existence of an organization. Strategic plans differ from operational plans in terms of their time horizon, scope, and degree of detail.

David (2004), refers that strategic planning is long-term planning that focuses on the organization as a whole. The author indicates that the management of strategic planning goes through knowing the concept of strategy. It comprises a set of actions established on the basis of a coordinated plan; in order to achieve the objectives projected by the organization.

In the same way, in the opinion of the authors analyzed, the changes that have been experienced in society and in the economy have generated important mutations, bringing with them new paradigms in the way of exercising management, such as the use of tools strategies, which have been successfully applied in all sectors, through the use of tools such as: SWOT Matrix and Management Indicators.

It is necessary to emphasize that to introduce ourselves in the study of strategy, it is important to know that its origin dates from ancient times in the military field. Subsequently, the dynamism in the growth of organizations, the expansion and globalization of markets, which brings with it competition and the need to survive in different scenarios, makes its appearance in business organizations.

According to Chandler (1962) cited by Francés (2006: 23) the strategy is "The determination of the basic long-term goals and objectives of the company and the adoption of courses of action, and allocation of resources, necessary to achieve those ends" . Two aspects stand out from this definition, firstly "basic long-term objectives" and the second, which refers to the company in general without identifying whether it is public or private. In addition to the concepts expressed above, there are other approaches to define the strategy, as is the case of Kaplan and Norton (2004: 31 who mention that:

An organization's strategy describes how it tries to create value for its shareholders and customers. If an organization's intangible asset represents more than 75 percent of its value, then the formulation and execution of its strategy requires that the mobilization and alignment of intangible assets be explicitly contemplated.

Consequently, the strategy has different approaches depending on the field of application. This is how reference is made to strategic planning and strategic management, in the same way some authors refer to strategic management applied to small businesses, corporate strategies and strategic management in government organizations and non-profit entities, among others.

On the other hand, Kaplan and Norton (Ob. Cit) point out:

The Strategy is not a stand-alone management process, but rather is a step in a logical ongoing process that mobilizes an organization from a high-level mission statement to work performed by administrative and customer service employees. (p.61) Likewise, as mentioned above, it is important to consider that one of the most used tools in strategic planning is the SWOT matrix (weaknesses, opportunities, strengths and threats). In this regard, Serna (2008: 185) points out: "The SWOT analysis is designed to help the strategist to find the best coupling between the trends of the environment, the opportunities and threats and the internal capacities, strengths and weaknesses of the company".

Formulation of objectives in strategic planning

Goals are the foundation of any management program. The mission clarifies the purpose of the organization to management. The objectives translate the mission into concrete terms for each level of the organization. For Chiavenato (2006), the organization "consists of a series of components projected to achieve a particular objective, according to a specific plan." In this definition there are three important points: purpose or objective towards which the system is projected; the project or layout of the components; and the inputs of information, energy and materials, destined to make the organization work. (p. 15).

Every organization has some purpose, some notion of why it exists and what it is going to do; therefore, the mission, objectives and internal environment that the participants need, on which they depend to achieve their goals, must be defined.

Chiavenato (2006) affirms: "if you have no notion of what your mission is and where you are going, you run the risk of drifting and it will be the conditions of the moment that determine what you should do. She will be obliged to accept what others decide and not what she determines ". (p.15). According to the aforementioned author, "the objectives are the points towards which companies direct their energies and resources. If the organization is a means to achieve the ends through the capacity of individuals, the objectives are collective goals that represent socially significant aspects "(p.15). It is worth mentioning that the objectives are usually considered in terms of actions to be achieved, which are operationalized with specific tasks assigned in each of the hierarchical levels of the organizations.

Educational organizations are social units that pursue specific objectives: their reason for being is to serve those objectives. In the criterion of Chiavenato (2006), the objectives are related to what the organization wants to achieve, that is, it refers to the development that it hopes to achieve through its actions. Educational organizations are not objective-oriented entities, almost everything in organizations is oriented towards a goal, purpose, future state or result to be achieved. Each organization defines its own organizational goals.

As expressed by David (2008: 5):

> Strategic management is the science of formulating, implementing and evaluating decisions that allow an organization to achieve its objectives, it focuses on integrating administration, marketing, finance and accounting, production and operations, research activities and development, as well as computerized information systems, to achieve the success of the organization. Said author uses the term strategic management as a synonym for strategic planning, the latter term is the most common in the business world, while the former is more frequent in the academic field.

Likewise, Membrado (2013: 5), establishes that: Every company that competes does so according to a strategy and that said strategy can be developed in an explicit way, through a planning process or implicitly, due to the interaction of the activities of the functional areas. The emphasis given to strategic planning by the companies with greater positioning, reflects the fact that the benefits of carrying out an explicit strategic planning are greater than implicit, since it ensures, at least, that the policies of the functional departments are coordinated and directed towards the same objective.

Similarly, David (2008: 5), defines it as strategic management, in this sense, a position is established with the author since strategic planning is a diagnostic, analysis and decision-making tool, which is situated in what to do current and the path that organizations and institutions must travel in the future, to adapt to the changes and demands imposed by the environment to achieve maximum quality in their products and services. The process of developing an internal analysis is a process in which strengths and weaknesses of the organization or the functional area of the business are identified.

David (2008: 122) from his point of view establishes that the internal evaluation should focus on identifying and evaluating the strengths and weaknesses of a company where all functional areas such as administration, marketing, finance, accounting, production, are included. operations, research and development, as well as management information systems. The relationships between these areas and the strategic implications of the important concepts of the functional areas are evaluated.

Serna (2008: 167), presents as an internal evaluation an analysis that consists of evaluating their present situation. According to the aforementioned author, in the business world there is no standard definition of what auditing an organization is. Each company determines the focus as the depth of diagnosis it requires to review and update its current strategy.

Similarly, Membrado (2013: 41) establishes that in the allocation of resources, the organization must manage its financial resources in support of its policy and strategy. For this, the global planning process is essential, where financial planning will be an important step in short and long-term planning, and therefore will support the organization's policy and strategy. Thus, the organization demonstrates its support by allocating budget items to finance training, improvement team programs, recognition, salary and promotion policy, among other important aspects.

As time passes, strategies become obsolete, which is why the importance of constantly evaluating the strategy, in this sense David (2008: 336), defines that: the evaluation of the strategy is essential for the well-being of an organization; Timely evaluations allow management to be alerted to current or potential problems before a situation becomes critical. Strategy evaluation includes three basic activities: 1. examine the underlying foundations of a company's strategy, 2. compare expected results with actual results; and 3. take corrective action to ensure that performance is according to plans.

For their part, Thompson, Peteraf, Gamble and Strickland (2012: 37), indicate that the formulation of the strategy is an effort that includes administrators in various positions and organizational levels. Formulating strategy is sometimes not exclusive to senior executives. They also set the task of devising a strategy that involves solving a series of "hows": how to grow the business, how to satisfy customers, how to be better than rivals, how to respond to changing market conditions, how to manage each part functional business, how to develop the necessary capabilities and how to achieve strategic and financial objectives.

The strategy formula is a transcendental stage because it is where functions of great interest are performed, it is where the responsibility of devising the strategy is acquired, David (2008) describes what management is and the strategic perspective is the key point to formulate the tactics because the main idea of the organization is reflected in them, it should be noted that it is necessary to do both an external and internal analysis as this way the opportunities, threats, weaknesses and strengths that the organization has can be identified in order to institute planning in the same way appropriate to the environment surrounding the organization.

The objectives are exact to obtain the success of an organization because they establish the direction to follow, help in the assessment, create synergy, reveal priorities, guide the coordination and provide a basis to carry out with vigor the activities of planning, organization , motivation and control. The objectives must be challenging, easy to evaluate, permanent, reasonable and clear.

As a ploy

The generation of new businesses in the current context requires being very innovative, understanding innovation as the creation of an effective value proposition that attracts customers. The most important thing in the company or organization regardless of its activity is the ability to generate business, although without a doubt, there are no mature companies but managers and entrepreneurs lacking imagination. All this way of thinking can be called at the discretion of the researcher, entrepreneurial management and affects as necessary entrepreneurs and company managers.

Therefore, all these entrepreneurial initiatives must pursue economic and social stability. However, the strategic principle applies stratagem, war ruse, pretense and contrived deception as a means used with skill and skill to achieve something.

Regarding this synthesis, Lanier (2011) points out that "strategy from the point of view of entrepreneurial management owes much of its misunderstood fame to what should actually be understood as a stratagem". It is actually part of the application of strategic logic, it is a guiding principle of action, but in no way replaces the understanding of strategy, much less of the strategic.

It then happens, in the opinion of the authors, that entrepreneurial management as a stratagem constitutes the most important representation of strategic thinking, by giving the stratagem a privileged position among strategic thinking. This, however, has not received the same appreciation and attention among exponents of contemporary strategic thinking. The latter have always privileged big movements and action.

These reasons are supported by Dorr (2008), when he points out, on the one hand, that the application of stratagems is vital for the effectiveness of the strategist, it is the raison d'être of entrepreneurial management because each of the actions that are being developed are It is skillful in taking into account the key elements of the entrepreneurial process. The ploy is based on pretense and deception, misinformation or manipulation of the same. The stratagem is a concrete plan of action that is only clear and makes sense in the mind of the Strategist.

Accordingly, Méndez (2007) consider that the stratagem "consists of pretending that something is being done, when in reality something else is being done, it consists of making believe that one thing is being thought, when in reality another is being thought. ".

That is, the stratagem seeks to make the opponent see what you want him to see and not necessarily what he should see. By means of a stratagem, the information that is wanted becomes evident, the rest not, until the moment when reality cannot be reversed by the adversary.

Strategic modeling

According to what was expressed by Acevedo et al, (2010), the strategic model, such as planning, is one of the initial actions of any organization, formed for the development of human activity, where essential elements are established that in the administration They are known to foresee the future and examine performance, in order to create habits for coexistence and growth of individuals in the activities to be carried out in the organization.

On the other hand, Suárez (2016) affirms that the strategic model is based on creating actions aimed at strategic planning, to analyze the processes that contribute to identifying elements in the organization, in order to align them, among them: the philosophical elements of the organization, made up of the mission, vision, values and corporate image, and in this way to be able to address opportunities and weaknesses as feasible strategies for the implementation of new actions in the environment.

From the perspective of Cano et al (2008), cited by Villamizar and Pelekais (2015), the strategic model is one that illustrates the planned planning process, including the strategic and marketing nature, taking into account the perception of some authors about those elements that they consider important, to understand everything related to the management of the same (organization), and in this way conceptualize the selection of variables that may prevail; especially in the definition and creation of plans in order to be formulated, evaluated and implemented, understanding that the models are abstractions of the reality where the individual develops, in order to reveal a purpose.

Villalba (2006: 75), for his part, defines it in stages, with a business approach, whose formulation of competitive strategies is given by the analysis of structures, followed in order by competitive advantages, the third would be on the strategy model to implement. In this sense, it determines the plans directed by actions that lead to the purposes designed and intended by the organizations, which according to the aforementioned author would be the fourth and fifth stage to be implemented in the creation of a strategic model.

According to Kenneth (2000), in organizations its main objective is to align the processes to achieve purposes, plans and objectives, which determine the strategies, essential in management and this can contribute to the benefit among competitors in addition to being able to demonstrate potential or skills.

It complements what was expressed by Jaramillo (2000: 16) who defines competitive strategies as the conduct of actions that allow advancing and extending solutions for the company in relation to competitiveness in addition to the design of how the objectives can be with respect to the desired purposes; that is, the aforementioned author defines them as the combination of strategies or goals that determines the company to strive to achieve the purposes. Likewise, it gives you a focus from three perspectives, competitive strategies, focus differentiation, and cost leadership.

Finally, David et al (2003), define the strategic formulation, as that mission in which the processes developed by the companies are established, to determine the necessary objectives, which is the direction or consecutive scope of the organization. Therefore, it must be understood by each of the members and be defined by specific guidelines.

In the same way, higher education organizations among the philosophical elements is the mission as an essential indicator, for the development of activities in order to achieve the objectives proposed in the processes and allow the identification of strengths, weaknesses, with the consecutive objective of effective management.

Strategic direction

All organizations have the same reasons to justify their existence: grow, provide a service or product, generate profits. That is, they clearly define an organizational purpose. However, organizations have to go beyond these basic reasons, if they want to differentiate themselves in the market (Serna, 2012), expressed in other words, having defined their strategic direction, which is integrated by corporate principles, vision, mission and overall objectives of the organization.

Likewise, the aforementioned author refers that a strategic planning process begins by identifying and defining corporate principles. In this sense, each organization is unique because its principles, its values, its vision, the philosophy of its owners, its collaborators and the groups with whom they interact in the market are different for everyone. This difference is reflected precisely in the definition, in the purpose of the organization, which is operationalized in the vision.

In the same order of ideas, the mission constitutes, according to Serna (2012), the formulation of the purposes of an organization that distinguishes it from other businesses in terms of the coverage of its operations, its products, markets and human talent that supports the achievement of these purposes, the vision is the set of general ideas, some of them abstract, that provide the frame of reference of what a company is and wants to be in the future. It must be broad and inspiring and, like the principles and mission, must be known to all employees of the organization.

Strategy formulation

The task of devising a strategy involves a series of "how-tos": How to grow the business, how to satisfy customers, how to be better than rivals, how to respond to changing market conditions, how to manage each functional part of the business, how to develop the necessary capacities and how to achieve the strategic and financial objectives. It also means choosing from a variety of strategic options, proactively searching for opportunities to do new things or to do the same in a new or better way. (Thompson, Peteraf, Gamble and Strickland, 2012).

In this sense, Saloner, Shepard and Podolny (2011), state that if the strategy evaluation reveals problems with the current strategy of the organization, the next step is to determine what other strategic options the company has. Each of the options must be a coherent and independent strategy that contains the four elements of long-term goals, focus, competitive advantage and logic.

Likewise, Serna (2012), argues that the strategic options should become concrete action plans, for this it is essential to project each of the strategic projects over time, define the objectives and strategies of each functional area within these projects strategic. These, and the action plans must be reflected in the strategic budget, which in short, is the true strategic plan.

The strategic budget must be executed within company standards, monitored and audited as an important part of strategic planning. According to Chiavenato and Sapiro (2011), there are three requirements that are imposed on the strategic planning process: objectives, strategies and actions. A crucial aspect of this process is its preparation, which must be carried out by people who interact and discuss with each other, in addition to exchanging ideas and negotiating with each other, until reaching a match regarding the policies decided.

Taking into account what the authors propose, the researcher concludes that they have coinciding points such as the definition of objectives, strategies and actions; However, Serna (2012) goes further, when he states that action plans must be supported with a strategic budget, that is, that ensures the financial resource for the execution of the strategies formulated.

The performance of an organization must be monitored and audited. To do this, based on the objectives, action plans and strategic budget, some indices will be defined that will allow measuring the performance of the organization. This measurement will be carried out periodically, so that it provides timely feedback to the strategic planning process and, therefore, the adjustments or modifications that the situation requires can be introduced.

In this sense, the formalization of this process of periodic evaluation and measurement institutionalizes the strategic audit, a fundamental component in the creation and consolidation of a strategic culture. This audit as a system ensures the persistence, permanence and continuity of the process, avoiding that strategic planning is just a fad, which lasts very little.

Functional objectives

Based on the statement of the organization's mission, based on what is referred to by the authors Chiavenato and Sapiro (2011), a hierarchy of objectives is proposed, in which the broadest, or the organizational or strategic objectives, which consider the results expected of it as a whole.

Likewise, Serna (2012), proposes that the conjunction of global objectives and the strategies that are defined for each objective, will integrate its corporate strategic formulation for the company. This is specified by establishing each of them in a concatenated way. This author affirms that these objectives are the integrating factors of the task of senior management and therefore should be reflected in the functional and operational plans of each strategic business unit.

In the same way, Chiavenato and Sapiro (2010), state that the organizational objectives are broken down into the business objectives of the divisions or business units and these, in turn, are divided into functional objectives by areas or departments (objectives tactical), until establishing the objectives for teams and people (operational objectives), thus creating an integrated and convergent whole at all levels of the organization.

Strategic projects

Projects are of fundamental importance to identify, in addition to the inputs and outputs, the resources and information necessary to ensure good performance. According to Chiavenato and Sapiro (2012) it is the way of projecting the means with which the organization intends to produce and deliver its superior quality products and services to its clients. They are implemented at all levels of the organization.

In this regard, Serna (2012) outlines that strategic projects are the result of analyzing the strategic options and giving priority to each of them, selecting those in which they must have an exceptional performance as a condition to achieve their objectives, and therefore Hence, its mission and vision.

From this perspective, these projects must be explicit about the consolidation of strengths, attack weaknesses, take advantage of opportunities and anticipate the effect of threats; consistent with the overall objectives and mission. Therefore, they must point towards those objectives and therefore, towards the vision, be absolutely necessary and consistent with the business. Thus, each objective should focus on one or more strategic projects.

Similarly, strategic projects must be few but vital, no more than five, in order to facilitate their monitoring and control, and dynamic, that is, lead to action, therefore, they should not start with the word " We must "or" We need ". At this stage of the process, those responsible for the strategic projects must develop the action plan to achieve the proposed results expected within the previously defined time horizon.

Paraphrasing Serna (2012), it is important then, to take into account that in order to develop strategic projects, the strategies that are the activities that will allow the scope or realization of each project must be specified.

For the selection of strategic projects, the following must be taken into account: (a) The corporate vision and mission. Consistency with the mission of the company and its contribution to the achievement of its vision; (b) The corporate objectives, by virtue of which they allow and facilitate the achievement of these; (c) That they point to little vital projects. They must target areas in which the company must perform exceptionally to ensure its success in the marketplace. They are those areas in which "things have to go very well."

In addition, they can coincide with functional areas or cover cross-functional activities. Therefore, strategic projects must be the result of senior management consensus on priority areas of concern. It can then be argued that strategic projects are related to the entire organization and it is essential to develop a correlation matrix to analyze the consistency between them, the functional areas and the global objectives.

Strategic alignment

Strategic alignment is the process by which an organization builds a shared vision and makes it a reality in the daily management of the company. The communication of the strategic plan to the entire organization will make the collaborators identify their responsibility in the execution of the plan and commit to it. For Serna (2012), the alignment of strategies, processes, people and the client with the strategic plan will ensure a shared vision. This is the key to strategic success.

In this regard, Quesada (2005), argues that it is a continuous "process" of linking the different elements of an organization towards the Organization's strategy and seeking a common vision and mission for all people. As a "process", it is capable of being defined, evaluated and consistently improved. It means synchronizing all the processes of the Value Chain of an organization, towards the achievement of the strategy and value proposition for customers, employees and shareholders.

Typology

To make strategic alignment a reality in the daily management of the company, three types or categories of alignment are taken into account: vertical, horizontal and integral. Vertical alignment is the set of programs and actions that an organization carries out to ensure that its collaborators know and incorporate the company's strategy.

For example, the activity carried out by a company to disseminate its strategic plan to the entire organization, with the objective that all its members know the direction of the organization; commonly used workshops and events are strategic to achieve this first stage of a business vision shared by all members of an organization.

Horizontal alignment seeks to make processes compatible with the needs and expectations of customers. To do this, companies define the business value chain, identify its key and support processes, and integrate them with customer needs and expectations. Serna (2012) points out that to achieve this alignment objective, organizations review their processes, eliminate value destroyers, and reengineer said processes. Knowing the customer is the point of improvement of these processes.

In this type of alignment, each of the business units, departments and areas, work to achieve common goals or system goals, those that each and everyone believes are important, which support the achievement of the objectives and goals of the Organization and contribute to achieving the expected results. (Quesada, 2005).

According to Serna (2012), independently vertical and horizontal alignment do not achieve the comprehensiveness required by the strategic orientation of an organization. A shared vision is only achieved when the strategy, processes, collaborators and clients are fully aligned. These processes are called integral alignment. When an organization makes efforts to achieve only one of the alignments, it wears out and does not reach all the efforts to have a single orientation and objective.

Strategic modeling aimed at entrepreneurship

From the Global Entrepreneurship Monitor (GEM) perspective (2012) in Spain, despite the fact that entrepreneurship is growing, the dedication that has led to new business ideas is remarkable. The important thing is not to put aside the execution of actions, but how expendable it is in organizations and entrepreneurial individuals have the necessary strategic tools to direct the proposed objectives.

Ricart (2009) explains that the design of a business model determines a set of functions carried out by the company, by which it proposes a plan or method that unites the actions by means of a tool that provides this perspective, such as the table of comprehensive command. On the other hand, Burbano et al (2016), define an entrepreneurship model through the value chain being a systemic model, which allows visualizing the perspective for decision-making and thus having a reflection of the future of everything that happened from past experiences up to the present, to reverse them and contextualize them in future actions.

In the same way, habitual thinking is not enough to drive systems over time; that is, the present thoughts are everyday and simple, so it is necessary to combine the elements of the present and the future to obtain possible favorable results.

Likewise, the national government with the application of Law 1014 of (2006), its main concern at the time was not the implementation of entrepreneurship in companies, but the construction of new guidelines that contribute to strengthen weaknesses in order to establish activities in the organization and determine new knowledge by entrepreneurs for the structuring of educational processes.

For this reason, the concern of the State as such is not only the immersion of entrepreneurship in the formation of the educational sector but the way in which it can be carried out in the application of the functions, in such a way that it encourages a directing of a model through the use of strategies that provide systemic actions aligned with what is intended according to the processes of the HEIs.

Therefore, the government implements through the creation of an entrepreneurship fund, whose purpose is to provide resources to those individuals who have business ideas, in order to emanate financial resources to support the innovative project as proposals presented by entrepreneurs, which They envision situations of opportunities in the environment.

Chapter Five: Let's Talk Entrepreneurship

According to Urbano and Toledano (2008) it is a way of thinking, reasoning, acting, linked and raised by the search for a business opportunity. For his part, Robbins (2005) calls it an entrepreneurial spirit and conceptualizes it as the process by which an individual or a group commits their organized efforts in the search for opportunities to create value and grow, satisfying desires and needs through innovation and differentiation, regardless of available resources.

Trujillo et al (2008) consider that entrepreneurship has gained interest for business schools since the eighties, for linking both business creation and management, among other reasons. This term is associated with the ability of a person to make an additional effort to achieve a goal or objective, it is also used to refer to the person who started a new company or project, a term that was later applied to entrepreneurs who were innovative or added value to an existing product or process.

In this way, in virtual environments like Gerencie (2011), entrepreneurship is defined as that attitude and aptitude of the person that allows them to undertake new challenges, new projects; it is what allows you to go one step further, to go beyond where you have already arrived. It is what makes a person is in constant search of new achievements beyond those he has achieved.

For Vainrub (2006), entrepreneurship consists of identifying opportunities, which are external, and obtaining the material, technical, economic and human resources to give body and soul to what was initially just an idea.

Guédez (2003) can also be cited, who states that from a conceptual point of view, entrepreneurship as such is the action of sniffing, capturing and identifying in the natural environment where the individual develops and taking advantage of opportunities offered by the environment.

Similarly, Bernal and others (2002) point out that the action of undertaking is undertaking, starting a work, a company, starting, doing. It's about committing to having an entrepreneurial attitude. And in this sense, the actions of young people should be practiced taking into account the activities to achieve the objectives set by themselves. According to the Instituto de Libre Empresa (2007), the entrepreneur is a person who has a business idea and who perceives it as an opportunity offered by the market and who has had the motivation, drive and ability to mobilize resources in order to to go out to meet new ideas.

Likewise, this type of person is capable of undertaking a project that is rejected by the majority, he knows how to interpret the real characteristics of the environment despite the fact that these are sometimes not apparent to his competition. On the other hand, you can fight against any inconvenience that comes across in your strategy and you are not afraid of failure. In addition, he is empowered to create a motivated group that gives it the required structure.

In this sense, each of the authors consulted, Vainrub (2006), Güédez (2003), Bernal et al (2002) and even the Instituto de Libre Empresa, agree that there is no prototype of an entrepreneur, everyone can Like what you do, you must have a passion for what you do. This passion must be present in everything, both in the general conception of entrepreneurship and in its day-to-day life. You must have initiative and recognize the initiative of others. An entrepreneur must be willing to risk more and receive less today, hoping to risk less and receive more tomorrow.

Entrepreneurial Management

Its purpose is to ensure that all participants in the management process harmoniously integrate the efforts in achieving the objectives set and with the aim of optimizing the work of all management in an ideal way. In this sense, management is directive action, which shows the behavior assumed by leaders to exercise dominance over others, through direct relationships with the group, highlighting communication, as an element that allows the achievement of excellent management ; proving essential in organizations to perform administrative functions.

In addition to the situation, Barceló (2007: 245) defines entrepreneurial management as:

The ability to create, train and initiate a project through the identification of ideas and business opportunities, analyzing exogenous factors, such as economic, social, environmental and political; as well as endogenous factors such as capacity in human, physical and financial resources which is carried out by dynamic people who have skills in communication, leadership and a positive attitude, offering alternatives to improve the quality of life through micro-businesses and job creation.

Therefore, it is essential for the existence, survival and success of organizations. In this management the situations are very diversified. No two organizations are the same, just as there are no two identical people. Each one has its objectives, its field of activity, its managers and staff, its internal and external problems, its market, its financial situation, its technology, its basic resources, its ideology, its business policy and a number of others. factors that differentiate it from the others.

According to Sánchez (2008: 153), entrepreneurial management "implies that the human factor is the first and most important cause of success", which is why the social approach is recognized as useful and applicable to study the behavior of the individuals that make up an organization, this means that every institution is productive to the extent that it achieves its goals. In other words, it implies interest in effectiveness and efficiency in the work performed.

In correspondence with the author of the reference, Jaimes (2009) states that the entrepreneurial spirit of management is essential for the functioning of market economies. In these economies, entrepreneurs are the vectors of change and growth and can help accelerate the creation, dissemination and application of innovative ideas. The new business dynamics are closely linked to the integration of companies in networks, their power and capacity for articulation, which demands the development of a new entrepreneurial entrepreneur profile.

On the other hand, Becerra and others (2007: 4) state that "the theoretical role of entrepreneurial management is to forge the tools of an operational action. It must provide efficiency, effectiveness and operability ".

Likewise, it states that this management comprises a set of procedures, rules and regulations, validated by practice with a strategic direction, which, when deployed in the organization, is systematically shaping the organizational structure.

In this sense, entrepreneurship management can be conceptualized, according to the vision of Robbins (2005), as the development of a project that seeks a certain political, economic or social purpose, among others, which also has specific characteristics, essentially which has a share of innovation and uncertainty.

This definition can be complemented with the proposal of Bruna (2006), who explains that entrepreneurship management is radical, discontinuous change or strategic renewal, regardless of whether it occurs inside or outside the existing organization, or if this renewal gives or not place, to the creation of a new business. Likewise, Vásquez (2015), expands that when it is managed based on entrepreneurship, it is therefore about pursuing the opportunity even beyond the resources currently available.

According to the above, it can be deduced that entrepreneurship management is carried out by means of a person (entrepreneur), who starts a company, although, it can also be associated with anyone who makes the decision to carry out a Although the project does not have economic purposes, it can be said that the difference between the entrepreneur and a common individual is attitude.

It should be considered that entrepreneurship management is executed according to Leiva (2009), by an entrepreneur with the ability to create, capable of carrying out his ideas, taking risks, generating goods and services, facing problems, therefore it has to be an individual who knows how to see and discover opportunities even in difficult and unstable situations. Management makes the entrepreneur have his own initiative, also creates the structure he needs to promote his project, he communicates easily, generating communication networks, since he has the capacity to convene and even if necessary knows how to form high-level work groups functioning.

In relation to the implications mentioned above, Vásquez (2015) points out, that an enterprise has the characteristic of being innovative, which means introducing a change, this can occur in several ways, including in the social structure, in the development of a product, in public management or in the organization of a company, among others. Robbins (2005) explains that this innovation implies a path through which knowledge is transferred, becoming a process, a product or a service that adds new advantages for both the market and society. It should be noted then, that although innovation can be present in any sector, it is characteristic of the business sector.

In this regard, Heredero et al (2013) express that the innovative individual sees change as a norm of life, although it is not necessarily the one who brings change, however it is who seeks it, responds to it and exploits it as an opportunity, In short, to innovate is to see what everyone sees, to think what only some think, but to do what no one does. In relation to all the above, it can be indicated that entrepreneurship management generates the idea of the existence of an entrepreneurial spirit, coupled with the ability of a society to produce and assimilate changes, convinced that these are favorable for growth and economic development . In short, this entrepreneurship management refers to factors and qualitative changes in the life of the individual and of the society in which they coexist and coexist.

Entrepreneurial management approaches

From the field of private universities, Moenaert (2010: 78) refers that the need to train people with transversal skills is well known so that they become a versatile professional and be able to form their personal criteria, fundamentally for entrepreneurship and culture. business. Parallel to the training of people, Domini and Domini

(2012: 10) state that it is also necessary to have effective and flexible institutions, which allow bringing the private rate closer to the social rate of benefits, minimizing the transaction costs implicit in development of markets and organizations.

Therefore, it is necessary to generate policies aimed at adapting and reforming private universities to encourage the potential for entrepreneurship. In the same vein, Barceló (2007: 76) that entrepreneurial management as a business approach, "constitutes a continuous process of problem solving, decision making, strategy development, process improvement, among others." For this reason, every organization is permanently subject to a series of pressures that force it to react and respond to new events, in markets as dynamic and changing as the current ones, in times of uncertainty and globalization.

Consequently, entrepreneurial management approaches spearhead the capacity, attitude of people and companies to form combinations and in turn associations, relationships or restructure elements of their reality, achieving original and relevant products or results. That is, to have new and useful ideas, to know the importance of effort, perseverance with enough imagination to alleviate the fatigue of the road and savor the syrup of triumph in advance.

Opportunities to create entrepreneurship

This point begins with what was raised by Urbano and others (2008: 45), cited by Robles and Pelekais (2015), who point out the entrepreneurial process is that process that integrates all the functions, activities and actions associated with the identification and exploitation of opportunities.

Hence, the need to mention that to undertake it is necessary to assume an attitude based on the values that the individual has, since both the risk and the economic gains, sacrifice or dedication, are characteristics attributed to the exercise of entrepreneurial activity.

In this sense, as stated by the aforementioned author, entrepreneurship as such could take place in new or old, small and large, slow or fast growing projects or companies, within the private sector, the non-profit sector or within the public sector , in all points of the geography and stage of development of a country, however, in addition to the entrepreneurial activity that a person develops on their own initiative from a business idea, other manifestations can also be addressed, such as: franchises , family businesses, social businesses or within a company already established intrapreneurship (p.37).

Seen this way, the opportunities to create entrepreneurship arise at certain moments and must be taken advantage of to avoid later regret. The important thing, therefore, is to be attentive to those that are presented in any field and analyze them to determine which is the most convenient option, which may mean the possibility of a promotion, a hiring offer or the proposal to start a new project or entrepreneurship.

Increasingly, the word entrepreneur appears associated with the idea of opportunity, Leiva (2009: 52) states that "they are individuals dedicated to the search for opportunities, beyond the resources they have available," so an opportunity defines it as those "situations in which new products, services, raw materials, markets and organizational methods can be introduced through the formation of new means, ends or new means-ends relationships".

It is convenient to know that according to Quintero and Sánchez (2005: 123), in order to consider an idea as a business opportunity, it would be necessary to verify the existence of: "potential customers, who buy products, with unsatisfied needs; with partially satisfied needs, dissatisfied with their current "supplier" and some who do not even know that they need what they want to offer and without forgetting who can buy without even needing it ".

On the other hand, to create an entrepreneurial opportunity, according to the authors, "personal feasibility should be considered, since opportunities do not exist in the abstract for all people equally, not all opportunities are for everyone", and some skill must exist. in order to satisfy that need. Also, clients with resources are required, that is, clients who can pay.

All of the above reflects that by taking advantage of the individual's potential in their ability to recognize the opportunities that arise, they can generate entrepreneurship, also using strategies such as seedbeds, forums, ideas contests, business plan, diagnosis of the situation and competitive advantages; as a starting point for the innovation of the management of organizational processes, considering that group work, creativity, crisis resolution and information management are some of the relevant aspects when it comes to training entrepreneurs.

Strategies to develop research based on entrepreneurship management

Valverde (2011) points out that the constant variations that arise in the social aspect, bring as a consequence a kind of demarcated meanings due to imposing systems such as the economy, culture, education; For this reason, it is precisely in this last aspect that diverse natures are linked in relation to the abilities, competences or axiological notions in the very practice of social support. In this way, large companies bet on studies delimited by factors, trends or variables, seeking the best position regarding the productive dynamics of the market.

This is how research appears in the technical, business and financial scenes, seeking, according to Torrent-Sellens (2014), to solve those problems concerning the economic spectrum, since, as companies become increasingly global in the Supplying markets, research, of markets for example, becomes more useful to marketing managers. Of course, when talking about an investigation focused on entrepreneurship, then Vásquez (2015) refers that the intervention of the academic scene in eminently quantitative groups of a fluctuating market stands out, which by not finding effective answers to its phenomenology, appeals to the epistemology of business research.

Unlike some positions on research based on entrepreneurship, Bruna (2006), bets on the methodology that must confine itself to pragmatic fields, where this concept is complicated by its nature undermined in forgotten projects; Therefore, research as a practice to establish links with business reality, irgue its importance because of entrepreneurship as an economic, labor and professional possibility since it is a way of thinking and acting oriented towards the creation of wealth.

Heredero et al (2013) argue that research is a way of thinking, reasoning and acting focused on opportunities, raised with a global vision and carried out through balanced leadership and the management of a calculated risk, therefore that its result is the creation of value that favors the company, the economy and society. In accordance with this, in a world surrounded by labor competencies, as well as technical skills, these imply a look at the possible results, aiming to economically favor the entrepreneur, in this panorama it is seen how research assumes a role in sociological studies, rational and quantitative that appeal to the resolution of complex problems such as the positioning of a certain brand, the bankruptcy of a company, others.

From the perspective of Valverde (2011), entrepreneurship has been spoken of as a set of actions that demand internal solutions, based on a possible economic reengineering whose fate is represented by concepts such as SMEs, development, skills or sustainable growth, here, It is where a possible object of study for research lies, delimiting holistic dimensions to get ahead, progress or create solutions to problems that impede the effective development of man.

After the previous considerations, the author assumes the fact that research is not only about the diagnosis or the deteriorated result in statistical figures, investigating the demand for theoretical and methodological categories implemented with innovation to undertake epistemological processes, which causes the apprehension of a reality semantics in the economic context, such as the very act of undertaking.

Another way of putting it is proposed by Heredero et al (2013), who affirm that entrepreneurship and research can be found in the same contexts as the creation of academic scenarios, for example business schools or lines of research in business careers. Entrepreneurship and research as systematic structures then, are integrated into the conceptualizations of the academy, where they are based on the current situation of a reality, understanding different qualitative and quantitative positions where the phenomenological fights not to continue falling into superficial relativisms In terms of employment or sustainable development, this is the importance of research in entrepreneurship.

Seedbeds of entrepreneurship

According to what is stated in the EPM Foundation Manual (2014), cited by Robles and Pelekais (2015), the Seedbeds are playful learning spaces, in which the student can develop entrepreneurial capacity and acquire key competencies to be an entrepreneur. Taking into consideration that group work, innovation, creativity, crisis resolution and information management are some of the relevant aspects when it comes to training male and female entrepreneurs.

Likewise, in its article 2 it establishes that they aim to:

Generate alternative extracurricular spaces, which allow the development of culture and entrepreneurial and research training in business, academic, scientific and technological fields, resulting in the generation of knowledge, business innovation among the members of the seedbed and impacting on a choice of grade.

One of its purposes being to generate alternative extracurricular spaces, which allows the development of culture and entrepreneurial and research training in business, academic, scientific and technological areas, resulting in the generation of knowledge, business innovation among the members of the seedbed and impacting on a grade option.

On the other hand, the way of creating entrepreneurship has changed, it is no longer the same as before, it is necessary to emphasize that it was a cultural change, where, first, a predominant factor in the academic field, related to philosophy, has to be addressed university based on the intellectual training of professionals, instead of serving as an intermediary for the creation of companies.

This is how Bonilla and Sánchez (2005) conceive it, the entrepreneurship seedbeds seek to develop the vision that "from the academy, professionals who may be the great models or the great anti-models are involved, so that the process of transformation and search that generates the creation of a company ". That is why a project that includes well-oriented aspects such as the development of a business seedbed for analysis and prior organization, mainly seeks to establish the concept of pre-incubation of the company.

With this strategy, according to Urbano and others (2011: 85), it is proposed to "stimulate, guide and advise the future entrepreneur, so that the real and concrete foundations are built, based on a business idea". For this to be possible, you must know what is the required capital, who makes up your clientele, how your competition is integrated, what needs you will be able to satisfy and, finally, what is the viability of your project.

The notion of the company that is managed emphasizes the stage prior to its materialization and then the moment in which the conception of the business idea is carried out from an entrepreneurial perspective, to visualize, in this way, the opportunity and define the action plan, based on the competencies of the entrepreneur who suggests it.

Key factors of entrepreneurship

For Frixone (2012) the key factors for successful entrepreneurship are: a) whoever starts a business must be clear that they will work more than eight hours a day, if they want to achieve the proposed objective; b) desire to get ahead; c) motivation to be free, independent, without bosses, without schedules; d) continuous training of the employer and workers; e) from the point of view of family financing, in-laws are the best financiers, brothers and brothers-in-law are bad financiers; f) use the knowledge learned as an employee of another organization when creating their own company, remembering that being a professional is not a requirement to create a company, which if it happens is that professional entrepreneurs start with an advantage.

Similarly, it is necessary to seek new business opportunities in what are basic needs, such as food, clothing, housing. Consider that strategic alliances are a good alternative. It is also necessary to achieve the goal set, use marketing techniques to expand markets, trying not to start in debt with a bank and above all be very responsible from all points of view.

According to Frydman (2003), among the factors that allow success in entrepreneurship are knowledge and analysis; combined with creativity to mix and combine these variables in a special way; in addition to the ability to execute or know what to do to execute the appropriate combination.

Correspondingly, for Husenman (2006), he points out three key factors in entrepreneurs, firstly being a hard worker, having a lot of energy put into work; secondly, stand out as very dynamic people, and finally, thirdly, be quite aggressive, when attacked, respond quickly, not with complaints but with actions. In short, according to the above, the success factors of entrepreneurs are due especially to personal characteristics, information and knowledge, adaptation to technological change and updating, as well as products.

Skills to undertake

According to what was stated by Pellicer et al (2013) when they refer that the concept of entrepreneurial initiative, entrepreneurial spirit or similar concepts in the educational environment refer to the development of personal qualities such as creativity, willingness to innovate, self-confidence, achievement motivation , leadership and resistance to failure, among others.

These qualities are necessary, as is regularly said, in any context and for anyone. They also point out that The key question is: Is the entrepreneur born or made? Social entrepreneurship

Authors such as Arce (2012), refer that entrepreneurship are the engines that drive the existence of expectations and the need or flight forward, in times of economic turmoil like the current one, where social entrepreneurs have an opportunity to become a true option in the country, create awareness and create jobs in various areas. It reinforces what was expressed by Reis and Clohesy, (2011: 116) who assure that social entrepreneurship is influenced by the desire for social change, the sustainability of the organization and the social services it provides.

Likewise, social entrepreneurship for Choi & Majumdar (2014) consists of adapting business strategies with the aim of contributing to social well-being. In this way, social entrepreneurship is understood as the creation of new products, services and business behaviors that, in addition to satisfying the needs demanded by society, supposes a sustainable social transformation (Dacin, et al., 2010).

For their part, Gatica et al (2012) refer to it as the process and opportunity to create value for society, generating a change or impact in the community, either through the creation of products and services, or through new models of businesses or new organizations, these activities are driven by the actions of an individual, a group or various organizations that operate in a given context.

In general, social entrepreneurship includes opportunities that add value to the development of communities through initiatives that help promote a better quality of life, for the common welfare of all.

They agree with what was stated by the aforementioned authors, Melian & Campos (2010), who consider that social entrepreneurship has three objectives: economic, social and socio-political. The first, referring to the economic objective, ensures that economic activity is sufficiently solid and that it has investment returns that allow it to be financially viable; The second objective of a social nature will be the labor inclusion of sectors with high risk of exclusion (work for deprived of liberty) or the provision of services to a group at risk of exclusion that allows them to finance their own businesses (microloans with low interests to poor sectors of Muhammad Yunus);

Dimensions of social entrepreneurship

This section explains the dimensions of social entrepreneurship, being a starting point to establish the criteria that support from the base of a commitment that adds value to the development of institutions and communities, being a practice that responds to the needs of society or the gaps in the market, with innovative proposals and sustainable financing, in order to solve the pressing problems of the communities, also counting on the cooperation between the public and private sectors and non-profit organizations. It is worth mentioning that among the elements of the social dimension the following are shown:

Social initiative

According to De la Cuesta et al (2003) within social initiatives there are some thematic axes which demonstrate the commitment that society has, in this way they have to do with the ethical-social approach that defines alternatives such as health, sport, education, employment and infrastructure are important issues with a serious and dignified commitment.

Social capital

Jaramillo (2003) states that they are a set of norms, trusts, values, attitudes, and networks between people and institutions in a society, which define the degree of associativity between the different social actors, facilitating collective and cooperative actions; The author points out that social capital has several dimensions, including an individual one, which contemplates the degree of integration into its environment from relationships with people, families, companies; a sectoral dimension, the action of people, families or companies in their sector or expanded environment, their interrelation and their relationship with public powers, this has to do with community networks, unions, associations, among others. Finally, the collective or national dimension has to do with society as a whole.

Reinforcing the above, Klisksberg (2003) affirms that social capital are samples of the wealth and strength of the social fabric of a society that allows benefits for people and society as a whole, in this case, it can be considered as a network whose nodes are individuals, institutions and whose use generates returns.

From the precepts of Novacovsky (2003), social capital can be divided into individual (access to information and assets, voice and participation, community (improvement of collective enterprises, access to collective goods and services) and societal (increase of enterprises, stimulates creativity, and mitigates risks of social fracture).

All that has been mentioned shows the importance of social capital to reinforce a culture of entrepreneurship, in which the active participation of all the actors who make an active life in a certain institution is required.

Individual characteristics of entrepreneurs from the perspective of their motivations

Independence

Independence is one of the most characteristic aspects of entrepreneurs. The vast majority of entrepreneurship theorists consider this factor in their analysis.

For Hisrich et al (2005), the need for independence is related to the need for control; entrepreneurs tend to do things their own way. Finding it difficult to work for others The foregoing coincides with what was stated by Urbano and Toledano (2008), for whom businessmen show a clear inclination for autonomy and independence, a fact that justifies, in part, their preference for becoming their "own bosses ". This manifests itself in a refusal to work under the orders of another person, or to be subjected to the rigidity of a schedule, a salary and a perfectly defined activity.

Furthermore, it manifests itself through the desire to launch their own ideas and initiatives. In this regard, according to Krauss, Frese, Friedrich and Unger (2005), the need for independence leads to an expression of individuality, which is manifested in the refusal to follow a pattern established by an organization; In short, it implies that entrepreneurs value their own decision-making and dislike taking orders from superiors.

Achievement

The need for achievement, developed by McClelland (1965), is another of the personality factors most widely considered in studies of entrepreneurship. According to this author, entrepreneurs show very high impulses regarding the need for achievement and power, but a low need for affiliation. This need leads individuals to set high goals for themselves, seeking excellence and accepting responsibilities.

For their part, Caldas et al (2009) support this theory and argue that achievement motivation implies the achievement of the proposed goals, incessantly in the pursuit of projected success, despite the failures and the risks assumed. From the business point of view, according to Robbins (2005), entrepreneurs have growth and profitability as their main goals. However, not all new companies grow, as many remain in the same place, either by choice or omission.

Power

Power is according to McClelland (1965) one of the most fundamental needs of entrepreneurs. In this regard, for Gasse and Tremblay (2009), those who love power are frequently animated by the desire to lead and influence. Specifically, these people show willingness to coordinate actions and control resources; similarly, they are attracted to maintaining a certain social status.

Risk-taking can be defined, according to Brunet (2009), as the propensity to commit to an action based on the probability of success, given certain possibilities of failure. It is closely related to the nature of the entrepreneurial spirit; however, it is often undervalued and encouraged.

In this sense, from the perspective of Lugo (2010), risks are not simply dangerous to avoid, but in many cases, opportunities to take advantage of. All economic agents, including business organizations, are subject to various types of risks, which show the degree of uncertainty about the occurrence of a random or fortuitous event that endangers the stability or health of the company.

In this regard, according to Caldas et al (2009), although the risk does not depend on the will and desire of the employer, it does imply a personal experience which could generate doubt and fear due to the obligation to make decisions and execute them, knowing in advance that the consequences could mean the probability of losses.

Risk, then, implies making decisions and assuming their consequences, evidence of the degree of uncertainty about the occurrence of a random or fortuitous event that endangers the stability or health of the company. In reference to the aforementioned, there are various approaches regarding how entrepreneurs take risks. According to Hisrich et al (2005), the acceptance of risks, whether financial, social or psychological, is part of the entrepreneurial initiative process.

In this, Caldas et al (2009) agree, for whom risk is inherent in entrepreneurial activity, since it takes place in an unpredictable environment, where many internal and external factors to the organization act, many of which cannot be controlled.

Opportunism

As Robbins (2005) refers to, entrepreneurship goes beyond the simple creation of companies; Being an entrepreneur necessarily implies being in a constant search for opportunities and having the ability to identify them. In this sense, it is about being an observer, analytical, while making timely business decisions.

Perseverance

Perseverance implies the willingness to insist despite failures or obstacles that may arise. According to Gasse and Tremblay (2009), perseverance translates into a constant determination to carry out efforts towards finding solutions to problems; it implies tenacity and responsiveness to adversity. However, according to Seligman (2006), perseverance does not imply the obsessive search for unattainable objects; on the contrary, you need to be flexible, realistic and not a perfectionist.

Self-confidence

Self-confidence is another of the qualities of entrepreneurs. According to Brunet (2009), on a personal level, the individual who seeks to improve their performance; it is conditioned to be more and more effective and the results influence self-esteem. In the face of adversity, according to Gruhl (2009), resilient people see themselves in a positive way, supported by the basic confidence of being able to mobilize their personal capacities and digest setbacks; Your self-esteem is, in essence, largely independent of outside influences.

Optimism

Heoptimism is a human being's disposition to take a positive stance in the face of events. According to Gruhl (2009), optimists and pessimists differ from each other by the way they see, feel and experience the world, their own person and others. When problems arise, optimists automatically activate their crisis management strategies; on the contrary, pessimists focus on the bleak aspects of the situation and future difficulties.

Creativity

Entrepreneurs must have the ability to produce different alternative solutions to the challenges and problems that arise. Koontz and Weihrich (2004) agree on this, for whom entrepreneurs have creative ideas, use their resources and administrative skills to satisfy identifiable needs in the market.

According to Urbano and Toledano (2008), entrepreneurs are people with a tendency to avoid normal paths, to enter a world full of uncertainty. In the business field, according to Hernández (2010a), being creative and imaginative could generate new growth horizons, not only in terms of the sale of products and services, but also in the possibility of becoming a supplier of excellence and effective. Entrepreneurs always look for alternatives and opportunities to generate income, even in times of crisis.

An example of this could be an entrepreneur who, although he does not have great economic and technological resources to impact advertising, applies his ingenuity, human talent and creativity to promote his offer, grow his sales and consolidate his portfolio of clients.

From the perspective of Gruhl (2009), creative thinking is required in crises, because new situations can rarely be controlled with the usual means. When obstacles appear, you have to find new paths and continually modify strategies.

Innovation

Entrepreneurs are always looking for alternatives and opportunities to generate income, even in times of crisis. An example of this could be an entrepreneur who, although he does not have great economic and technological resources to impact advertising, applies his ingenuity, human talent and creativity to promote his offer, grow his sales and consolidate his portfolio of clients.

From the perspective of Gruhl (2009), creative thinking is required in crises, because new situations can rarely be controlled with the usual means. When obstacles appear, you have to find new paths and continually modify strategies.

With regard to innovation, according to Koontz and Weihrich (2004), the entrepreneurial spirit implies dissatisfaction with the prevailing state of affairs and awareness of the need to do things differently. In this sense, Robbins (2005) affirms that entrepreneurship goes beyond the simple creation of companies; Being an entrepreneur necessarily implies being innovative and constantly searching for opportunities; it involves trying to change, revolutionize, transform or introduce new products or services, or new ways of doing business.

In this regard, according to Hisrich et al (2005), innovation is the act of developing something new and unique. The ability to create and understand, at the same time, all the influencing forces in the environment is required, so it is a complete matter.

Indeed, according to Brunet (2009), innovation can be inhibited by the perception that an original idea may carry greater risks. However, for Koontz and Weihrich (2004), innovation is not a matter of luck; It requires a systematic and rational work, well organized and aimed at obtaining results.

Business entrepreneurship

It can be approached from different perspectives: Gámez (2009), in his "approach to entrepreneurship models", managed to describe this variable from different approaches, concluding that the economic school offers an understanding of the entrepreneurial phenomenon from the actions of the individual to maximize the utility and achieve their well-being; on the other hand, the Sociological vision considers the individual and their relationship with the search for development, based on the creation of economic value.

However, in this work, business entrepreneurship was analyzed from the point of view of the human factor, for which it was sought to determine how the individual characteristics of the entrepreneur can be decisive in the processes of creation, maintenance and growth of a company, of in a way that makes it attractive for students to embark on the path of entrepreneurship as part of their life plan.

From an individual approach, according to Urbano and Toledano (2008), business entrepreneurship is a way of thinking, reasoning and acting linked and raised by the search for a business opportunity.

More broadly, Hisrich et al (2005) define entrepreneurial entrepreneurship as the process of creating something new with value, dedicating time and effort, assuming the corresponding financial, psychological and social risks, in order to obtain the rewards resulting from the financial and personal independence.

For his part, Robbins (2005), calls it "entrepreneurial spirit", defining it as the process by which an individual or a group commits its organized efforts in search of opportunities to create value and grow, satisfying desires and needs through innovation. and differentiation, regardless of available resources.

School entrepreneurship

As established by Jaramillo (2008), School Entrepreneurship is a capacity of human beings to get ahead in a novel way and with renewed ideas, the word entrepreneurship comes from the French "entrepreneus" which means pioneer; Therefore, school entrepreneurship is not only a unique and external vision of the teaching-learning process but, as an internal condition of education where education must facilitate the development of new personal skills, such as the ability to innovate, find creative solutions and adapt to change.

For the Universidad de los Andes (2009), School Entrepreneurship is the contribution of carrying out an idea and transforming it into a complete good or service, in addition to the ability to innovate, lead and satisfy any educational need or demands.

Likewise, Moncayo (2006), raises School Entrepreneurship as the way of thinking, reasoning and acting focused on opportunities, school entrepreneurship is vitally important for the development of education, promoting a comprehensive education of the human being. When comparing the approaches of Jaramillo (2008), Universidad de los Andes (2009) and Moncayo (2006), they coincide in some aspects of Entrepreneurship as something internal to the human being, capable of thinking and reasoning, but in the same way they differ in that School Entrepreneurship is not only a personal asset but also that it can be transformed into a public service.

Types of entrepreneurship

There are different types of entrepreneurship, in this part mention is made of each one of them and their conceptualization, among the concepts made are the ones mentioned below. For the Universidad de los Andes (2009), it is the way in which the world that faces today, as educators, demands to be consistent with a good performance as professionals, hence the types of entrepreneurship are role models.

According to Moncayo (2006), it indicates that the types of undertakings are independent aspects of the motivations that give rise to people to associate attitudes and behaviors linked to commitment and these are based on two aspects such as: Need and Desire.

Need

The entrepreneur by necessity is one who embarks on the adventure of starting up his purposes and projects, taking advantage of life opportunities that arise through his knowledge and his own vocation, facing the extreme needs that arise throughout his career . According to Moncayo (2006), due to life conditions he faces extreme needs and in the context of that urgency he discovers the soul of an entrepreneur and manages to get ahead.

The authors believe that today the need is one of the primary factors in education to develop entrepreneurial capacity in each of the students, resulting in the development of human and entrepreneurial skills to get ahead in all aspects of life.

Wish

The entrepreneur by desire is one who arises and seeks opportunities in life to get ahead with a formal training, dedicating their efforts and human skills to find new opportunities, using the resources and tools that are in their environment from there.

According to Moncayo (2006), he argues that it is a way of thinking, reasoning and acting focused on life opportunities that with a formal education dedicate their efforts and resources to apply their knowledge. The researchers believe that at the educational level, an entrepreneurial student by desire is one who maintains a way of thinking focused on the opportunities that arise, dedicating all his effort to achieve a goal and also achieve his proposed purposes throughout his life .

Entrepreneurship practices

Entrepreneurship practices It is common to find in today's societies a public sector that provides poor social services, at the same time, the private sector is often accused of having an unethical attitude, either with its employees or with its clients, and of caring little for the environmental and social effects of its activity. According to Monsalve (2009), entrepreneurial practices are born with the will to correct these deficiencies, they can be framed in the promotion of communication actions of the company with the community to strengthen relations. This also determines the ability to define a communication objective by generating a coordinated strategy on all the activities to be developed and whose relationship gives coherence to each and every one of these actions.

By Therefore, the aforementioned author raises the need to create a communication plan which can distinguish the benefit of incorporating all the elements by establishing a method with all the actors, including the involvement of the company for which said plan is developed. In this way, said enclosure will be essential.

Regarding what has been raised, Drayton (2005) points out that social entrepreneurs assume creativity as entrepreneurial practices and that they personally need to provoke a change around them. In addition, they are marked by ethical principles that generate trust in the people around them. Likewise, According to Drucker (2010), the people who carry out Social Entrepreneurship, assume as the north, the modification of the way society acts, transform through the detection of problems and the development of innovative solutions, as well as strengthen these initiatives manage to contribute new norms or social behaviors.

Based on the postulates of Monsalve (2009), Drayton (2005) and Drucker (2010), it can be stated that entrepreneurial practices establish for management management those actions aimed at compliance with the essential organizational principles which allow responding to the identified needs, these must be framed in the indicated options so as not to offer improvisation possibilities.

Sustainable entrepreneurship

Sustainable entrepreneurship is characterized by being a form of social, human and economic integration, in order to carry out business initiatives that allow the use of opportunities that arise in the environment, likewise it is identified by looking for the best way to produce goods and services that satisfy the needs of the community, incorporating creativity as well as innovation into its activity, another of its relevant characteristics is to take the individual as an added value of cooperation, for the integral development of the economic environment, thus achieving stability that ensure its sustainability.

This new vision of sustainable entrepreneurship due to its innovative nature, comes to displace the traditional conception where the benefit is taken advantage of individually,

Therefore, sustainable entrepreneurship will conglomerate a heterogeneous set of initiatives aimed at generating economic, social and ecological goods in parallel López, (2012). In other words, from the point of view of social research, sustainable entrepreneurship is assumed and identified as the process of studying who and how opportunities are created, ordered as well as exploited, to bring into existence future goods and services taking into account account of its economic, social and environmental consequences, Cohen and Franco (2005).

In this sense, Porras and Sierra (2010) point out that entrepreneurship, today, has gained great importance due to the need of many people to achieve their independence and economic stability.

The high levels of unemployment as well as the low quality of existing jobs have created in people the need to generate their own resources, start their businesses, going from being employees to being employers. Entrepreneurial development is a phenomenon of a systemic nature, the emergence and development of new dynamic companies requires that there be people with vocations and clear motivations to undertake, with business projects that have growth potential, with appropriate capacities to bring them to fruition. Two closely linked factors that affect the existence of motivated people as well as entrepreneurship skills are culture and education. Kantis, (2008).

Entrepreneurial spirit

Given the current conditions of the environment, managers must be concerned about continuous interaction with the environment and their rapid ability to respond to its demands in an innovative and creative way, that is why the entrepreneurial spirit has become a skill strategic management for the achievement of organizational success.

Therefore, Hernández and Rodríguez (2006: 261), refer that the entrepreneurial spirit "lies fundamentally in the ambition to progress, succeed and constant growth, which can be reflected above all in the use of knowledge and professional training".

This is why Formichella (2009: 227) states that the entrepreneurial spirit is defined as "the ability to use differently those that already exist, in such a way that a significant impact is generated, through the need to achieve and innovation and the positive character towards the achievement of the proposed goals ". It can be indicated that the entrepreneurial spirit is understood as a way of thinking, reasoning systematically and acting focused on strengths and opportunities, raised with a global vision and carried out through balanced leadership and the management of a calculated risk.

On the other hand, David (2008: 249), argues that the entrepreneurial spirit "is the ability to take advantage of individual capacities to visualize existing problems as possible opportunities for improvement". For this, the manager must have a broad vision of the strengths and weaknesses of each of the members of the organization, in order to take advantage of them in transforming the problems presented into potential opportunities.

Likewise, Camero and Cerquera (2007: 243) define the entrepreneurial spirit "as a vital force with which it is driven towards the accomplishment of great things, acting in a decisive, innovative and motivated way in such a way that the proposed goals are objectively fulfilled. and thus to be able to achieve success, turning organizational problems into opportunities for improvement and improvement ".

In this regard, Lussier and Achua (2009: 252) define the entrepreneurial spirit as: The managerial ability as that human condition that allows perceiving social opportunities in order to achieve their objectives, through constant motivation and the ability to mobilize a series of resources in order to find this opportunity and materialize it in obtaining the desired goal Similarly, the author highlights essential elements in the entrepreneurial spirit such as managerial skill of the manager, the capacity for innovation, the capacity for motivation and responsible work, the spirit of improvement and perseverance and the visualization of problems as opportunities for improvement.

In another order of ideas, according to Gutiérrez (2012) the ideal factors for the emergence of the entrepreneurial spirit are: freedom, education, the environment and a strengthened institutional setting. These four components described by Gutiérrez (2012) are detailed below:

- Freedom is one of the components for the birth of an entrepreneurial spirit, taking into account that the attitude of every entrepreneur involves starting, investigating, taking risks, they are only possible in an environment of freedom, since only he can give the opportunity not to place any limits on ideas and give way to creativity, in order to really take advantage of opportunities.

- Education is another factor that undoubtedly exerts a great influence on the formation of an entrepreneurial profile because it allows us to envision opportunities and analyze existing resources, in addition to achieving the link between these aspects.

- The environment or the environment in which an entrepreneur works is one of the also important factors, in the sense that it is there where the entrepreneur develops. In many places an entrepreneur is promoted as a leader and as a positive force in society, however there are places where the entrepreneur faces a totally different horizon where he is rather restricted.

The time and effort established by entrepreneurs will manage to change the perception of society in relation to the value involved in entrepreneurial activity. The institutional scenario is also essential to favor the birth of the entrepreneurial spirit because it regulates economic and social activities, being essential a solid scenario that manages to project a future with clear established rules, in addition to generating access to information since it it is essential for decision making.

Entrepreneurial vision

For Hernández et al (2015), the entrepreneurial vision is considered highly relevant in all areas of society, it is especially significant among young people, characterized by their creativity, innovation, entrepreneurial and adventurous spirit, less fear of risk and greater sensitivity towards technological changes, which make them better candidates to carry out this type of project.

Adding, in the same way, the referenced authors that vision is understood as the place where we want to go, how we see ourselves in a certain time, then then the entrepreneurial vision is the future projection of a person as an entrepreneur with an established business and with success. The above is probably the visualization of an entrepreneur whose company has established itself and has grown in the market (Trias, 2007). Therefore, the development of this type of vision in university students is an important task of higher education institutions, for which the design of strategies for this purpose is the task not only of the management, but also of a group of people dedicated to the task of developing an entrepreneurial culture that promotes business vision.

Entrepreneurial motivation

Sastre (2013: 2) refers to the fact that entrepreneurial motivation, to a greater or lesser extent, has been present throughout the history of humanity and seems to intensify and flourish mainly in periods of globalization.

For this reason, entrepreneurial activity, either out of genuine interest or necessity, is important if we consider the economic and social health of a society. From the social point of view, because it provides opportunities to work and create jobs and, from the economic point of view, because it contributes to the generation of wealth (Torres Carbonell, 2010). It is for this reason, among others, that in societies in general, it is common to find support mechanisms for entrepreneurial activity.

Chapter Six: Walking the methodological path

The research reflects the position of the researcher in his representation and origin of ideas, which is based on epistemology, in which he establishes a position through a context, described through questions and answers to the situations presented in the problem from a scientific study.

In this sense, it requires a methodological perspective, considering different arguments in the different elements of the social environment and the people within the organization, who are the ones who determine the techniques and analysis of the data obtained in order to establish the procedures, to explicitly contextualize knowledge.

In epistemological studies, it is the direction of a position in order to establish the cognitive action associated with the capacity of the individual in the determination of generating knowledge by the researcher, giving an approach that involves from the personal to the cognitive for the advancement of study. Given the epistemological orientations, it describes the Gnoseological and ontological perspective of the researcher.

In this order of ideas, Parra (2005) defines that knowledge is born from the interrelation between what is investigated and whoever investigates; which generates knowledge to immerse itself in the presented reality that is the object of study to understand its subjectivity and intersubjectivity, obtained by the means and instruments used, whose purpose is to know human realities in environments such as positivism and post-positivism .

It is important to highlight that the research is born from the observed reality, by allowing the analysis of strategic modeling as a management platform in the competitive development of entrepreneurship in Higher Education Institutions, which addresses the phenomena that are tied as a direct influence of the study. Therefore, the research includes the interaction of the situations between the object of study in relation to analyzing knowledge, beliefs and culture, from a position, allowing to understand the position of the person, objectivity and subjectivity of the study, in addition to visualizing the different edges of knowledge, through the experiences obtained by the staff.

From what has been said, it is evident that this research is qualitative, with a postpositivist approach of a phenomenological, hermeneutical nature, where ontology prevails; since it surrounds the being in the investigation as such in the environments, with deep analysis to try to determine the truth of the actions leading to fulfill the established purposes, for the development of an entrepreneurial culture leveraged in a strategic modeling. Designed in certain stages called moments, which are essential elements that allow the study to be strengthened, in order to achieve the outlined purposes.

Basing the above with what was stated by Arias (2008), when he points out that the post-positivist approach focuses on the understanding and description of the subject, which is concerned with the existing realities of individuals in organizations to reveal the meanings implied in actions, beliefs, motivations, among other characteristics as an unobservable fact that is directly susceptible to experimentation.

In this order, the research includes the interaction of the situations between the object of study in relation to analyzing knowledge, beliefs and cultures from a position, allowing to understand the position of the person and the objectivity and subjectivity of the study, visualizing the different edges of knowledge through experiences obtained by staff.

According to Sandin (2003), he defines post-positivism as social facts of a holistic and interpretive nature, which assume the roles of the environment as elements of meaning for the interpretation of social behaviors, that is, the human being determines his human behavior in social contexts and originates its causes according to the actions attributed to reality, therefore, it allows theoretical constructions giving rise to a causal explanation.

Polit and Hungler (2012) cited by Mendoza and Fernández (2012), from a holistic perspective, the paradigms are represented by a vision of the global world given its complexity in the orientation of the questions from the philosophical point of view, finding methodological questions.

For this reason, the teaching processes can be determined in different ways of thinking in a knowledge society, whose characteristics, cultures and social aspects have a direct impact on the individual, all of this oriented towards investigative thinking.

For León (2009), phenomenology allows establishing a philosophical reflection that establishes the objectivity of knowledge through methods aimed at rules in actions to contextualize the compendium through which things are presented, placing a judgment on their validity and interpretations about the researched. In the same way, phenomenologies determine the necessary bases for the analysis and construction of theories of knowledge, based on the understanding and perception of the researcher in order not to get involved, making the phenomenon subjectivity that allows him to establish a value judgment being critical in a constructive way to reality.

In this order of ideas, González (2013) defines knowledge as an epistemological paradigm that interprets textual information about individuals and their actions in the existing world, that is, phenomenology and hermeneutics try to explain daily actions, which they extract essential phenomena and concepts in research.

For all the above, the phenomenological from the hermeneutic allows creating knowledge from the constructive and non-constructive, in order to determine the truth. However, it seeks to transcend through the perception of the pure fact with respect to what is intended to be explained, starting from the hermeneutic.

According to Maturo (2007), it defines the phenomenology where man is the central being, the reason for the environment and the globalized; It is being with others, whose intention is to discover the actions of the subject and go beyond the transcendental, understanding the natural acceptance and the culture of individuals acquired according to thought. Which infers that man is the essence of being and surrounds everything that surrounds through actions, determines the direction of something with respect to the environment, that is, it is the interaction of being with being, it is the part where it reflects the posture of man from the physical, spiritual and space edges. It is the essence of ontology.

On the other hand, Natativa (2012) defines phenomenology as those acts or actions that determine the experiential form of people, that is, the very essence of what is studied and where it is intended to go. On the other hand, hermeneutics tries to understand the phenomena or actions incurred by individuals, due to the multiplicity of events whose purpose is to determine the interpretations transmitted by people to explain and describe the events.

With respect to gnoseology, he defines it as the search for the truth in the phenomena incurred by exploring, describing what is intended by knowledge, taking into account the perception of things from various points of view, such as the subjectivity and objectivity of the environment . However, the construction of knowledge depends solely and exclusively on the researcher. By another order of ideas, Axiology is the knowledge generated by the researcher respecting the existing reality, having a global perspective of the phenomena that have occurred.

Regarding the instrument used, it consisted of an in-depth interview with the twenty-five key informants, made up of two members from each of the research groups, two from the research center, two from the seedbeds, 05 professors and eight professors from plant; to collect the feelings and experiences of everyday life.

Chapter Seven: Results

The results show the need to formulate a model that integrates the actions that must be fulfilled for the development of an entrepreneurial culture in the university institution under study, based on the need to promote articulation between higher education institutions, a community where is anchored and the productive sector. In this way, the student can visualize the opportunities that the environment offers, preparing to tackle them, in the same way, it makes it easier for him to show which are the weaknesses to fill them, which contributes to promoting entrepreneurial attitudes.

These results coincide with the arguments outlined by Bermúdez et al (2011) when they affirm that one of the main topics of interest is the economic aspect and this is directed, on the one hand, in the reproduction of capital, through entrepreneurship strategies that contribute to the environment. .

In the same way, with what was indicated by Burbano et al (2016), who defines an entrepreneurship model through the value chain being a systemic model, which allows visualizing the perspective for decision-making and thus having a reflection of the future of everything that happened from past experiences to present ones, to revert and contextualize them in future actions.

In the same way, they coincide with what was stated by Gutiérrez (2015) who assures that within the framework of the University, Company and State (UEE) relationship in Colombia. The performance of the triad requires an in-depth analysis of the link between the business sector in the investigative instances. For this reason, the triad implies for the parties to deepen the matter and, clearly, to integrate the role of the investigation on said agreement.

Therefore, one of the aspects to be strengthened is the internalization of the values that promote entrepreneurship, such as honesty, solidarity, responsibility, excellence, exemplifying it in each of the subjects that are dictated with favorable and stimulating situations of student entrepreneurship. . Teach them how changes are made to achieve high productivity performance, through a specific project with some type of innovation.

On the other hand, it was also possible to corroborate that the main barriers to assuming new approaches favorable to growth generally rest on the entrepreneur himself and are related to fears of leaving a safe space for an adventure, especially in Latin American countries, in the which people are deeply rooted in their roots and affections, being the main challenges to overcome: fear of failure, fear of change.

Likewise, coinciding with what was stated in the final report of the project "Promotion of youth entrepreneurship in the city of El Alto", a strong resistance to the change of passive rate was identified, this is made visible as something desired, but also as something that can have negative effects on your life ("you don't live if you only think about having more"), which is why a cognitive dissonance occurs that could have an immobilizing effect on internal resources.

By way of suggestions

Generate strategic guidelines appropriate to the current and future needs of the Institution. To formulate them, aspects such as university politics must be considered with respect to strategic planning and the enunciation of management indicators, actions that must be executed and responsible for each of the activities to be carried out, considering the importance of responding to the Organizational complexity implicit in an institution of higher education.

Similarly, to achieve the proposed objective, a review of the curricular mesh of the careers is required so that the culture of entrepreneurship can be considered as a transversal axis in each of the subjects taught at the institution.

Based on what has been raised, the strategic guidelines to which reference is made are presented, considering what was stated by Pelekais et al (2015), who emphasize that guidelines will be understood as the set of specific actions that determine the form, place and mode to carry out a policy within a planning.

They also constitute an explanation or a direction of principles. Likewise, it is a plan or program of action that governs any institution. It is a set of measures, rules and objectives that must be respected within an organization.

Strategic guidelines to build a culture of entrepreneurship in the public university institutions of the municipality of Soledad Atlántico:

The true capacity of the entrepreneur and of an entrepreneur is to be able to face challenges, which is something constant that will be present at all times, and only those with the ability and ability to find solutions and alternatives will be the ones who succeed. And this will not be the one who continues to think that because of others, the environment, the state, the economy itself, it is that he has not been able to create his company. (Crestani)

General Purpose: Build a culture of entrepreneurship in the public university institutions of the municipality of Soledad Atlántico.

Specific purpose: Implement in entrepreneurship projects the knowledge, skills and abilities developed in academic programs.

Strategies	Actions	Where	How	theoretical foundation
Human development	Formed at: -competences basic -competences labor -competences citizens -competences business -Development of entrepreneurial capacities in the students	-Formal educational system -Non-formal educational system	Articulation with the Productive Sector	LAW 1014 OF 2006 (January 26) Acevedo et al (2010) Burbano et al (2016) Cano et al (2008) David (2003) Kenneth (2000) Global Entrepreneur ship Monitor (GEM) (2012) Jaramillo (2000) Ricart (2009) Suarez (2016) Villalba (2006) Ardenghi (2001) Ackerman & Cervilla (2007) Alemany (2011) Bermúdez. J and others (2011) Villamizar and Pelekais (2015)
Increase	Redistribution of resources	Venturesinfor mal	-Family activity -Culture of cooperation	
Market	-Entrepreneurship using strengths - Neutra lize weakn esses	Tertiary markets	-Perceiving the context -Planning alternatives - Rep lyin g quic kly -Versatility in decisions -Flexibility to change -Imagination and intuition -Getting gradual and continuous financing -Planning strategically	

Positioning	-Implementation of differential strategies -Support for entrepreneurial initiatives	Target market	-Innovation -Creativity -Negotiation -Strategic Alliances	
Practices	Business creation exercise	Public university institutions of the municipality of Soledad Atlántico	-Characterization of the target market -Viability study -Analysis of the main functional areas of a company -Implementation strategies -Structure of the business plan	
Encourage ment and motivation	-Organization of Entrepreneurship Awards and competitions - Publications that spread entrepreneurial culture and good practices - Guidance and support in the creation and consolidation of Business	Public university institutions of the municipality of Soledad Atlántico	-Incubation, Nurseries, Technology Parks - Coaching and mentoring - Exchange networks with consolidated companies: real or virtual	

Epilogue

The expected results show that a model should be formulated and developed in agreement with the university authorities, in which strategic actions are planned to achieve progress on a topic as controversial as it is justified in any university, is the case of building an entrepreneurial culture from modeling strategic.

On the other hand, in terms of fostering a rapprochement between the university institution and the productive sector, as part of the model for strengthening the triad, the interest shown by business organizations anchored in the surroundings of the university to participate in a active and leading in the activities promoted to strengthen the culture of entrepreneurship that they are starting and aspire to strengthen; However, it is necessary to create the optimal conditions for this aspiration to go from an idea to a concrete fact.

In this order of ideas, the research that generated this product was initially focused on implementing strategic modeling as a management platform for a culture of entrepreneurship in public university institutions in the municipality of Soledad Atlántico. However, in the course of the study it was shown that each of these categories by themselves merited a thorough analysis, which is why we reviewed with the authors consulted the support generated in order to socialize these results.

On the other hand, it is important to highlight that in order to guarantee that entrepreneurship as a policy of the institution is successful, a series of guidelines are proposed, which must be considered within the planning formulated, involving different key actors in the process such as such as: the student community, teachers and researchers, university authorities, government entity that regulates the educational service, the community and the productive sector.

For this, the use of resources is necessary: financial technology, human talent, scientific and empirical knowledge, incorporating creativity, culture of innovation and ingenuity for the performance of the activity, for this reason, it is relevant that people have the strong conviction of their capabilities, therefore, it is essential that university authorities get involved by providing accompaniment and support in all stages of the development of the enterprise.

Another important guideline is the establishment of links between companies and the institution, to create interaction strategies that promote the creation of business initiatives that satisfy the needs, responding to the requirements of society, exchanging knowledge, experiences that guarantee the strengthening of the development of a culture of entrepreneurship with economic, social and innovative impact.

Bibliographic

Acevedo. TO; Linares; Cachay O, (2010), Model of analysis and strategic formulation. Employing Matrix Tools, Journal of the Faculty of Industrial Engineering. Peru.

Ackerman, B (2007) The Chair of Entrepreneurship as a Strategy for the Creation of an Entrepreneurial Culture at the University VII National Meeting of Curriculum I International Congress on Quality and Innovation in Higher Education.

Alemany (2011), Learning to Entrepreneurship, how to educate entrepreneurial talent Edited by Fundación Príncipe de Girona / Aula Planeta.

Allen, K. & Meyer, E. (2012) Entrepreneurship Creating Business. Mexico: Mc Graw Hill.

Amaru, C. (2008). Administration for Entrepreneurs. Spain: Pearson Prentice Hall.

Arce, P (2012) Which and how many companies in the Financial Sector in Costa Rica carry out Social Entrepreneurship or have expectations of developing social enterprises and what efforts have been made to achieve them? Latin American University of Science and Technology Faculty of Business Sciences Master of Business Administration Emphasis in Operations Management.

Arias, F (2008) The research project. Introduction to scientific methodology.Fourth edition. Editorial Episteme. Caracas.

Barceló, G. (2007). The leader of the future. Madrid Spain. Association for the advancement of leadership

Becerra, E. (2007). University transformation and Interuniversity

Relations: Non-extendable needs. Paper presented at the Universidad se Reforma IV. Caracas Venezuela.

Bermúdez. J .; Lascaris. T and others (2011), Entrepreneurship and innovation for the construction of a social capital. National University, Costa Rica.

Bonilla, L. and Sánchez, G. (2005). Innovative entrepreneurship and micro-businesses.Editorial UOC Business School. Barcelona, Spain

Brunas, J. (2006). The University facing the challenges of the knowledge society. Paper presented at the Universidad se Reforma IV, Caracas,-Venezuela

Burbano, R (2016), System Dynamics Model for Entrepreneurship Management, Emprender Fund –SENA, Valle del Cauca.

Bracho, K. (2013) "Entrepreneurship: Tool for Innovation and Competitiveness". Memories VII National and IV International Research Conference of URBE. Maracaibo. Venezuela Available at: http://www.urbe.edu/portal-biblioteca/basesdedatos-urbe/ponencia/.

Camero, V. (2008). Innovative Leadership Paradigm. Compilation. Madrid Spain. Editorial Mc Graw Hill.

Cano, M (2008) Some Planning Models. Veracruz University.Mexico.

Cavalli Sforza, LL (2007) The evolution of culture: concrete proposals for future studies. Barcelona: Anagram.

Cohen, E; Franco, R. (2005). Social Management: How to achieve efficiency and impact on social policies. First edition by 21st century editores, sa in co-edition with the united nations. Mexico

Cuervo, A. (2003). Analysis and Financial Planning. Madrid. Editorial Civitas.

Curto, M. (2012). Social Entrepreneurship: Structure, Organizational, Challenges and Future Prospects. Notebook No. 14. Spain: IESE Business School.

Chiavenato, I. (2006). Administration in the new times. Bogota

McGraw Hill Publishing House.

Chiavenato I. and Sapiro, A. (2011). Strategic planning. Fundamentals and applications. Edition No 2. Editorial Mc Graw Hill. Mexico.

Chirinos, Y. (2013). Sustainable Entrepreneurship as a State Policy. CITY. Maracaibo. Venezuela Available at: http://www.urbe.edu/portalbiblioteca/basesdedatos-urbe/ponencia/. Consultation made on 12/30/16., At 10:00 am

Choi, N, & Majumdar, S. (2014). Social entrepreneurship as an essentially contested concept: Opening a new avenue for systematic future research. Journal of Business Venturing, 29 (3), 363-376.

Dacin, P A., Dacin, MT, & Matear, M. (2010). Social entrepreneurship: Why we don't need a new theory and how we move forward from here. The Academy of Management Perspectives, 24 (3), 37-57

Donini, Y; Donini, J. (2012). Entrepreneurship and business creation: Theory, Models and Cases. Bogota Colombia. Editorial Universidad de la Salle.

David. s / f (2003) Concept of Strategic Administration. Ninth edition. Editorial Prentice. Hall-Mexico.

David, F. (2004). Strategic management. Mexico. Editorial Prentice Hall.

David, F (2008) Concepts strategic management. Eleventh edition.Pearson education Mexico.

David, N. (2008). Boss for the first time. Business leadership training. Madrid,-Spain. Macro Editor.

De la Cuesta, M. and Valor, C (2003). Social responsibility of the company, concept, measurement and development in Spain. Madrid. ICE Economic Bulletin

Del Pilar, M (2011) Entrepreneurship education: Strengthening entrepreneurial skills at the Pontifical Universidad Javeriana Cali. Javeriana university. Economy, Development and Management Magazine

Dorr, JM (2008). Educational Innovations and New Paradigms.

Department of the didactics of school organization. New contributions. Barcelona, Spain. PPU editions

Drucker, P. (2010) "The discipline of innovation". Harvard Business Review. 76 Plurinational State Bolivia and the United Nations Program for the

Development (2013). Final report of the project "Promotion of youth entrepreneurship in the city of El Alto". Available at: https://info.undp.org/docs/pdc/.../BOL/Informe%20Final%20B OL%2087104. docx

Evans, L (2012) Integrating Business Unit Strategies Into a Synchronized Corporate Strategic Plan. Retrieved from: http://blog.vistage.com/business-strategy- and-management / integrating-business-unit-strategies-into-a-synchronized- corporate-strategic-plan /, dated May 26, 2016.

Fernández, R (2009) Administration of corporate social responsibility.Spain. Thompson Ediciones international publishing house.

Formichella, N. (2009). Entrepreneurship Education: empirical findings and proposals for the design of entrepreneurship education concepts at universities in German-Speaking countries. Journal of Entrepreneurship Culture.

French, A. (2006). Strategy and Plans for the Company- with the Balanced Scorecard. Pearson-Prince Hall. Mexico.

Frixone, J (2012) Key success factors from the perspective of business entrepreneurs. I Entrepreneur Forum. Simón Bolívar Andean University. Ecuador. Available at: http://www.uasb.edu.ec/UserFiles/381/File/FACTORES%20CL AVE%20NE GOCIOS_1.pdf. Accessed 12/2/16

Frydman, F. (2003). Cultivate commitment. Fund development manual for social organizations. First edition. Buenos Aires, Argentina

Galindo, R; Echeverría, M (2011) Diagnosis of the entrepreneurial culture in the School of Engineering of Antioquia. EIA Magazine, ISSN 1794-1237 Number 15, p. 85-94. July 2011 School of Engineering of Antioquia, Medellín (Colombia)

Gámez, J. (2009). Approach to entrepreneurship models. Management, issn 0122-6681, Vol. XVIII, no. 31, January-June 2009, p. 153-170. University of San Buenaventura, Bogotá, DC

Garrido, F. (2007). Strategic thinking. The strategy as the nerve center of the company. Editorial Deusto. Spain.

Gatica et al. (2012). Social innovation in Chile and the role of the state in its development. School of Administration Pontificia Universidad Católica de Chile.

Manage. (2011). Entrepreneurship. Available at http://www.gerencie.com/empimiento.html. Retrieved 11/20/16.

Gibb, A & Hannon, P. (2007). Towards the Entrepreneurial university. International Journal of Entrepreneurship Education, Vol. 4, 73-110.

Guedez, V. (2006). Ethics and practice of corporate social responsibility.Editorial Planeta Venezolana. Caracas Venezuela.

Gutiérrez, J. (2015) Model of business investigative competencies from the university, business and state in Colombia. Prax. Know) [online]. Vol.6, n.12 [cited 2017-02-20], pp.241-267. Available from:

<http://www.scielo.org.co/scielo.php?script=sci_arttext&pid= S2216- 01592015000200012 & lng = en & nrm = iso>. ISSN 2216-0159.

Gutiérrez, H., López RAM, Luis J., and Amador M., Ma. E .: "The entrepreneurial potential in Accounting students at the San Marcos universities in Peru and Guadalajara in Mexico – Centro Universitario de los Altos –A comparative analysis "in Revista Caribeña de Ciencias Sociales, October 2012.

Haussman, R. (2003) Venezuela's growth implosion: a neoclassical story. In D. Rodrik ed. In search of prosperity, pp. 224-270. Pinceton University Press, Hernández and Rodríguez (2006). Administration and Management Development. Madrid Spain. Editorial Granica, SA

Hernández, C., Arano, R (2015) The development of the entrepreneurial culture in university students for the strengthening of the entrepreneurial vision. Administrative Science, 2015-1. Available   at:

http://www.uv.mx/iiesca/files/2012/10/04CA201501.pdf

Hisrich, R; Peters, M; Shepherd, D. (2005). Entrepreneurship. Entrepreneurs. 6th edition. Editorial Mc Graw Hill. Spain.

Jaimes, V. (2009). Human Talent through Competences. Bogota Colombia.Norma Editorial Group

Jaramillo, F (2003) The challenge to build social capital in Latin America.Caracas. Edited by Norma Color Caracas. Venezuela.

Kantis, H. (2008). Contributions for the design of National Entrepreneurial Development Programs in Latin America. Inter-American Development Bank. Vice Presidency of Sectors and Knowledge Social Sector Division of Science and Technology. Technical Notes # IDB-TN-132

Kaplan R. and Norton D. (2004). Strategic Maps- How to convert intangible assets into tangible results. Management 2000 Editions. Barcelona Spain.

Kenneth, A (2000) The Concept of Strategy in the Company. Mc Graw Hill. Klisksberg, B (2003) Social capital and culture. Forgotten keys to development. Caracas.

Leiva, JC (2009). Entrepreneurs and business creation. Technological Publishing House of Costa Rica. Costa Rica.

Law 1014 of January 26, 2006 to promote the Entrepreneurship culture. Ministry of National Education, Republic of Colombia. Retrieved December 16, 2008. http: // www. mineducacion.gov.co/1621/article94653.html

Law 1014 of (2006) From the Promotion of Entrepreneurship Culture. General Congress of the Republic.

Louffat, E (2010), Administration Fundamentals of the administrative process.Cengage learning Argentina.

Lowe, R., Marrot, S. (2012). Enterprise: Entrepreneurship and Innovation.Routledge. Oxford

Luengo, GE (2003). 'The re-founding of the university: relevance and viability from Latin America'. [ITESO, Mexico 1 Paper prepared for the International Conference at Universidade XXI, held on November 25-27, 2003, in Brasilea, Brazil, under the auspices of the

Ministry of Education and UNESCO]

Luna A. (2010) Strategic Management. First edition. Grupo Editorial Patria. Mexico.

Lussier and Achua (2009). Reflections and perspectives of Higher Education in Latin America. Final report. Tuning project. Latin America, 2004-2007. Spain: University of Deusto.

Martínez Rodríguez, F (2008), Doctoral thesis "Analysis of entrepreneurial competences of the students of the Workshop schools and Trade Houses in Andalusia. First phase of the design of educational programs for the development of an entrepreneurial culture among young people ".

Melián Navarro, A., & Campos Climent, V. (2010). Entrepreneurship and social economy as mechanisms of socio-labor insertion in times of crisis. REVESCO: magazine of cooperative studies, (100), 43-67.

Membrado, J (2007). Advanced methodologies for planning and planning improvement. First edition. Editions Díaz de Santos Madrid. Spain

Méndez, R. (2007). Entrepreneurship. An institutional development strategy. Madrid Spain. Editorial Neiva.

Mestres, L (2011) How to promote entrepreneurial culture. Available   at: http://www.educaweb.com/noticia/2011/05/02/como-fomentar-cultura- emprendedora-4748 /

Ministry of Education (2015). Review of National Policies in Colombia. Education in Colombia. Ministry of National Education (2011). The culture of entrepreneurship in educational establishments. Guide No. 39. Bogotá. Colombia.

Ministry of National Education of the Republic of Colombia (2010). Ten-Year National Education Plan 2006-2016

Mintzberg, H., Westley F. (2001). Decision making: it's not what you think. MIT Sloan Management Review

Moenaert, C. (2010). Management strategies for change in organizations.Barcelona –Spain. Editorial Amat Monsalve, A (2009)

Social Entrepreneurship Alternative Development Model. Bogota

Moreno, Z; Knight, A; Bastidas, E (2010) Strategic planning and the balanced scorecard: Management tools to improve the provision of university services. TEACS, YEAR 03, Issue 05, December. Venezuela. Novacousky, I (2003) Social Capital and applied ethics in development projects. Caracas.

Ohmae K. (2004). The Mind of the Strategist. Ed Mc Graw Hill.

Ornelas, C; Estela, C; Contreras González, L; Silva, M; Liquidano, Ma. Del Carmen. (2015). The Entrepreneurial Spirit and a Factor that Influences its Early Development Technological Awareness, no. 49, January-June, pp. 46-51 Technological Institute of Aguascalientes. Aguascalientes, Mexico

Páez, N. and Casas, N. (2012). Colombian business entrepreneurship. Editorial EAE. Santana, Boyacá, Colombia.

Parody. G (2015) Ministry of National Education- MEN-QUALIFY. Printed by Sanmartín Obregón Cía. Ltda. Bogotá, Colombia.

Pasten, F (2005) Technological Education Learning Sector. 1st course. Medium Pelekais et al (2015),

Pelleicer, C; Álvarez, B and Torrejón, J (2013). Learn to undertake. How to educate entrepreneurial talent. Available at: http://www.cise.es/wp- content / uploads / Aprender-a-emprender-C% C3% B3mo-educar-el-talent- emprendedor.pdf. Accessed January 2017.

Peraza, A (2014) Proposal of a socially responsible strategic management model based on electronic government. Graduate work, University of Carabobo. Barbula. Venezuela.

Pérez (2011) Entrepreneurship as a management strategy in educational institutions. Memories VII National and IV International Research Conference of URBE. Maracaibo. Venezuela Available at: http://www.urbe.edu/portal-biblioteca/basesdedatos-urbe/ponencia/.

Porras, J and Sierra, Ó. (2010). Approach to entrepreneurship from the perspective of innovation: the case of SMEs in Bogotá DC Received: October 4, 2010. Approved: December 16, 2010. Gestión y Sociedad. Magazine, Volume 4 No. 1; 43-61, January-June 2011, ISSN 2027-1433 Universidad de la Salle Colombia.

Posada, E (2013) Culture of entrepreneurship in rural indigenous educational centers of Colombia and Venezuela. Degree work. Private University Dr. Rafael Belloso Chacín. Venezuela

Quesada, G. (2005). Strategic alignment, key in the implementation of the BSC. Available at http://www.gestiopolis.com/el-alineamiento-estrategico- clave-en-la-implecion-del-bsc /. Resuscitat ing the Hospital Business Model »(in English)..

Quintero, A. and Sánchez, I. (2005). Entrepreneurship: a look from history to know its origin and evolution. Surcolombiana University. SME Research Group. Colombia.

RedEmprendia (2014) The promotion of an entrepreneurial culture and the improvement of training in entrepreneurship and innovation. Spain. Available at: https://www.redemprendia.org/sites/default/files/descargas/Info rmesREDEM PRENDIA1_El-Fomento-de-la-Cultura-Emprendedora.pdf

Reis, T. and Clohesy, S. (2011). Unleashing new resources and entrepreneurship for the common good: philanthropic renaissance. New Directions for Philanthropic Fundraising, 2011 (32), pp. 109-144

Revista de Educación (2015) The Strategic Management of Higher Education Challenges and Opportunities. Madrid Spain. Quarterly Magazine.

Ricart, J. (2009). "Business model: The missing link in strategic direction." Universia Business Review, 23: 12-25.

Robbins, S. (2005). Administration. 8th edition. Editorial Prentice Hall. Mexico Robles, A; Pelekais, C (2015) Entrepreneurship and management of organizational processes. Spanish Academic Editorial. Madrid

Rojas, G; Quintero, L; Pertuz, V; Navarro, A (2016) Strategies for the promotion of the culture of entrepreneurship in the universities of Valledupar, Colombia. Vol. 10, No. 1. Education and

Social Development Magazine. Pp 38-57

Red. G; Quintero. L (2015) Strategies for the Promotion of the culture of Entrepreneurship Universities of Valledupar, Colombia. DOI: http://dx.doi.org/10.18359/reds.1448.

Saloner, G; Shepard, A. and Podolny J. (2011). Strategic management. Editorial LImusa wiley. Mexico.

Sánchez, ME (2008). Measuring the impact of science and technology on social development. Presentation at the Workshop on Indicators of Impact of Science and Technology on Social Development, organized by RICYT, Mar del Plata, Argentina, December 12 at: http://www.scielo.org.ar. Consultation: December 12, 2016.

Serna, H (2008). Strategic management, Theory - methodology - alignment, implementation and strategic maps. Management indices. Tenth edition. Bogota DC

Serna, G. (2012). Strategic management. Edition No10. Editorial 3 R. Bogotá DC Colombia.

Schnarch, A (2014). Successful empowerment: How to improve your process and management. COE Editions. Bogota

Stoner, J .; Freeman, E. and Gilbert, J. (2006). Administration. Mexico. Editorial Prentice Hall

Suárez, F (2016) Strategic Management as a catalyst in the Organizational Success of MSMEs. Rafael Belloso Chacín University. Barranquilla, Colombia.

Trias F. (2007), The Black Book of the Entrepreneur: Don't say they didn't warn you, Editorial Empresa Activa, Barcelona, Spain, ISBN: 978-849-662-72-60

Thompson, A. Gamble, J. Peteraf, M and Strickland, A. (2012). Strategic management, theory and cases. McGraw Hill / Interamericana editores SA de CV. Mexico.

Thompson, A. and Strickland A. (2004). Strategic management. Texts and cases. Edition No 13. Editorial MC Graw Hill. Mexico

Torres Carbonell, S. (2010), "Global Entrepreneurship Monitor. GemArgentina Report 2009 ", available at:

http://www.iae.edu.ar/pi/centros/entrepreneurship/paginas/gem_reportes.as px

Urbano, D and Toledano, N. (2011). Invitation to entrepreneurship: An approach to business creation. Editorial UOC. Barcelona. Spain

Vainrub, R. (2006). Turn dreams into reality. A guide for entrepreneurs. IESA editions.

Vidal, J (2012) Promotion of culture and entrepreneurial spirit in young Spanish people from educational institutions. Cartagena

Villalba, J. (2003) The art of competitive warfare. Strategic menu. National Center for Competitiveness. IESA editions. www.uv.mx/iiesca/files/2012/12/modelos2008-2.pdf.

Villamizar, D; Pelekais, C (2015) Strategic management of business units as a prospective foundation of the Petrochemical Sector. Editorial PUBLICIA. Spain